BLITZ BRITAIN

MANCHESTER
AND SALFORD

BLITZ BRITAIN

MANCHESTER
AND SALFORD

GRAHAM PHYTHIAN

Front cover: Detail from photograph of firemen at work in Portland
Street during the December 1940 Blitz. (*Manchester Evening News*)

First published 2015

The History Press
The Mill, Brimscombe Port
Stroud, Gloucestershire, GL5 2QG
www.thehistorypress.co.uk

© Graham Phythian, 2015

The right of Graham Phythian to be identified as the Author
of this work has been asserted in accordance with the
Copyright, Designs and Patents Act 1988.

British Library Cataloguing in Publication Data.
A catalogue record for this book is available from the British Library.

ISBN 978 0 7509 6157 8

Typesetting and origination by The History Press
Printed in Great Britain

CONTENTS

ACKNOWLEDGEMENTS

My thanks go to the following:

Duncan Broady and the staff of Greater Manchester Police Museum and Archives, for access to wartime documents and loan of photographs.

Bob Bonner and the staff of Greater Manchester Fire Service Museum, for information on Salford, access to documents, and loan of photographs.

Andrew Schofield and the staff of the North West Sound Archive.

Dr Austin Elliott, for information on 'shelter legs'.

Tracey Walker of the Manchester Art Gallery.

Peter Turner and the staff of Salford Local History Archives.

Michael Powell, Canon Andrew Shanks and the staff of Chetham's Library.

Philip Lloyd for loan of ration books.

The staff of: Manchester Central Library Local History and Archives+, Trafford Archives and Local History, Stockport Local Heritage Library, Imperial War Museum North, Oldham Local History Archives, Salford Royal Hospital, Stockport Air-Raid Shelters Museum, Manchester Southern Cemetery, and Agecroft and Weaste Cemeteries, Salford.

John Clarke MBE KZ, Peter Dawson, Alan Eachus, Annie Gibb, Jerry Hartley, Francis Hogan, Jenny Johnson, David McCarthy,

Elizabeth McNulty, Ian Meadowcroft, Alan Morrison, John Nuralli, Eve O'Neill, Sandra Parker, William Paul, Olive Turnbull, Peter Wood, Constance Wright, and the late Dennis Humphries, for personal reminiscences.

… and of course to the team at The History Press.

Finally, every reasonable attempt has been made to trace the copyright owners of visual material used in this book. Any oversights or omissions should be communicated in writing to the author, c/o The History Press.

PREFACE

It has been said by wiser heads than mine that there is no such thing as a definitive history of anything. Herein lies the fascination: new details come to light, the accepted facts may be questioned, and there is always scope for fresh interpretation of what are currently the official versions.

So this book does not claim to be the final word on the Manchester and Salford Blitz of the Second World War. Also, many readers already familiar with the stories will no doubt recognise a lot of the details, and I have to admit that there is not a great deal that is startlingly new here (with the possible exception of some of the photographs recently brought to light by the Greater Manchester Police and Fire Service Museums). However, the rationale of the book has been to gather together, geographically and thematically, all the various narrative strands, with the accent on personal memories and oral history. It is the synthesis which I believe is new. And there is therefore some minor overlap with my *Manchester at War: The People's Story*, which may profitably be read as a complement to this work.

The books, documents and websites I consulted are given in the bibliography. The only sources I give in the text are for straight quotations, either from literature or newspapers, or from the direct speech of tape transcripts. Where no source for direct speech is given in the text, these are extracts from my own interviews or communications with the people involved.

In general I have based the narrative on primary sources, among which I would naturally include the testimony of the many contributors to the excellent Neil Richardson local history series. Where the primary sources have run dry or proven difficult to track down, I owe a sizeable debt of thanks to the work of Clive Hardy, Robert Nicholls, Stuart Hylton, Keith Warrender, Richard Overy, and Peter J.C. Smith (see bibliography).

A possible problem with wartime reporting is the existence of censorship. For reasons of security or morale, newspaper reports often give a vague, diluted or highly selective version of the facts. 'In war,

the first casualty is the truth', may be a cliché, but the more sophisticated the media, the more accurate an observation it seems to be.
I have used contemporary newspaper reports as a source, but wherever possible I have cross-checked the details from official documents,
a list of which I give in the bibliography and appendices.

I have indulged in a couple of instances of informed guesswork.
For example, I have placed the falling of the high-explosive bomb
on the grassy embankment described by Ken Harrop in Chapter
Four at the railway end of Trentham Street in Hulme. This is because
the location detail given in *Manchester Wartime Memories* is such
an embankment 'on the Trafford–Manchester border'. Having had
a good look round the nearby streets, and having consulted a contemporary map, I came to the conclusion that the Trentham Street
railway embankment was the only possible place for the bomb to
have fallen. I welcome corrections, if appropriate.

Parker Street and Portland Street warehouses from Piccadilly Bus Station,

The same goes for my opting for Mark Addy's bridge across the Irwell/Ship Canal as being the one crossed by Dr Garfield Williams on 23 December 1940 as he made his way across the blitzed city from Salford to Whalley Range. This footbridge was used later the same day by a family going in the opposite direction, from Sale to their home in Ordsall, so it seems fairly certain it's the same one, as by all accounts other major bridges were blocked.

I have included the well-known anecdote about George Hall receiving a custodial sentence for snoring in a public air-raid shelter, but I was unable to find a primary source for this. I would appreciate any enlightenment on the matter.

Dr Garfield Williams's words in Chapter One are from his article in *Our Blitz: Red Sky Over Manchester* (pp. 44-48). The quotations from John Clarke in Chapters Three and Five are from my recorded interview with him in August 2014. The Lord Haw-Haw extracts given in

23 December 1940. *(Greater Manchester Police Museum and Archives)*

Chapters Three and Seven are taken from my communications with people who recall the original broadcasts, and from oral recordings in the North West Sound Archive and the Salford Life Times archives. A full list of contributors is given in the acknowledgements.

The word blitz, of course, derives from the German *blitzkrieg*, or 'lightning war', which is an apt description of the rapid Nazi conquest of Poland, France and the Low Countries in the early months of the Second World War. As the pedants have pointed out, 'blitz' is therefore, strictly speaking, something of a misnomer when applied to the prolonged Luftwaffe attacks on British cities. No matter: the word has entered English usage, and now has a universally accepted meaning. Well, almost: 'The Manchester Blitz' may refer specifically to the raids of the two nights of 22–23 December 1940, or it may be used as a more general term, covering all the bombing attacks throughout the two years, even including Trafford Park, Salford and Stretford. This book's main emphasis is on the so-called 'Christmas Blitz' in these areas, but also includes detailed references to raids that took place at other times.

For readers unsure of the precise geographical demarcations: Salford is a city in its own right, quite distinct from Manchester; Trafford Park and Stretford are both areas within the Metropolitan Borough of Trafford, which is again separate from Manchester. Oldham, Bury and Stockport are also separate boroughs.

To clarify the location of Salford Royal Infirmary: the original SRI, the one that was bombed in 1940–41, was on Chapel Street. The exterior of the building has been restored, and there are flats on the site now. Hope Hospital on Stott Lane, also hit during the war, is now the site of the present-day Salford Royal, substantially rebuilt since 2007.

A footnote for those who might think that Chapter Nine overstates the praise for the city's renaissance: in 2014 Manchester was awarded the title of UK City of the Year by MIPIM (*Le Marché International des Professionels de l'Immobilier*) for 'major regeneration projects and attracting international investments'. Seventy-five years after the fires of the Blitz, the phoenix continues to rise.

• • •

For those unfamiliar with the British pre-decimal currency system, I offer the following guidelines:

One pound (£1) was divided into twenty shillings (20*s*).
A shilling was divided into twelve (old) pence (12*d*); so there were 240 old pence to the pound.
10*s* was therefore the equivalent of 50p, and 1*s* the equivalent of 5p.
'Seven shillings and sixpence' would be abbreviated to '7*s* 6*d*'.
'Ten shillings' would be written as '10*s*'.
A guinea was £1 and 1 shilling.

$$£1 \quad = \quad 20s$$
one pound   was divided into   twenty shillings

$$1s \quad = \quad 12d$$
one shilling   was divided into   twelve (old) pence

However, because of inflation, the modern equivalent of the sums quoted would be much greater. As a general rule of thumb, for everyday purposes multiply the 1940 cost by fifty to arrive at the 2015 value. This is not totally accurate for all commodities, as different rules of inflation have governed such areas as income, basic foodstuffs, luxury goods, property values, and Premier League footballers.

Graham Phythian, 2015

ONE

'A THING OF SHOCKING BEAUTY': THE FATE OF MANCHESTER CATHEDRAL

● IN THE FOOTSTEPS OF DR GARFIELD WILLIAMS, DEAN OF MANCHESTER CATHEDRAL, 22–23 DECEMBER 1940 ●

Before the Luftwaffe bombs dumped a large part of it as rubble across the northern end of Deansgate, Victoria Hotel was one of Manchester's most imposing buildings. One of a set of ornate and sumptuously appointed hotels purpose-built mainly to accommodate trade visitors to the city in the late nineteenth century, the Victoria occupied the fourth floor of a block which included select ground-floor shops and two storeys of offices. The plan of the block was roughly triangular, pointing north across a cobbled square towards Victoria Station. There was a glass dome at the St Mary's Gate end, and outside its apex stood the statue of Oliver Cromwell – the one which is now in Wythenshawe Park, facing the Hall.

The view northwards included the cathedral and Chetham's Hospital School, the former Manor House. Beneath the cobbles, by the confluence of the rivers Irwell and Irk, was the site of the Anglo-Saxon settlement of Mamceastre. Around the hotel block were the thoroughfares of St Mary's Gate, Hanging Ditch, and the medieval buildings of The Shambles. A few dozen yards to the north-west was the former Salford Bridge (now Victoria Bridge Street), which was the scene of the successful defence of the city against the Royalist cannon during the Civil War siege. History was writ large in those few hundred square yards, in many ways the spiritual heart of the city.

It was just after 6.30 p.m. on the evening of 22 December 1940 when the air-raid sirens sounded to give warning of an imminent attack on central Manchester. Dr Garfield Williams, dean of the cathedral, was in his room at the Victoria Hotel, jotting down some notes in preparation for the talk he was due to give at the Midland Hotel at lunchtime the following day. He usually spent Christmas week at the Victoria, so as to be close to the cathedral for the services. Because of the blackout restrictions, evensong had already taken place earlier that day, in the afternoon.

The dean's wife was staying with friends in Devon. For those Mancunians heeding recent developments, the attack on the city came as no great surprise. The war had been getting closer: London, Coventry, Sheffield, and then Liverpool the previous day, had all been put to the Luftwaffe sword. Persistent cloud cover over Manchester had been a protection for the best part of a week, but then Sunday the 22nd had been a crisp and clear day, and the full moon of eight days previously still afforded plenty of light to help the invaders navigate when night fell. With a significant number of the City Fire Brigade away at Liverpool to help combat the fires there, it was the optimum moment for the airborne attack to create havoc in the Manchester streets.

The usual method followed by Göring's and Hitler's favoured *blitzkrieg* assault on cities was to send in an initial wave of Heinkel 111s or Junkers 88s armed with thousands of incendiary bombs. The incandescent flames caused by these devices acted as a guide for the next wave of bombers, which were carrying the heavy stuff: the high-explosive bombs and the aerial mines.

Perhaps engrossed in his work, Dr Williams failed to hear the sirens, but was distracted several minutes later by a crackling, spitting noise – 'like fireworks'. It was the sound of incendiary bombs setting fire to the hotel and surrounding streets.

Stuffing his notebook into his hip pocket, Dr Williams hastily packed a bag and left his room. An auxiliary fireman informed him that the hotel had been hit by three incendiaries, and that people were being evacuated to the Grosvenor Hotel on the other side of Deansgate. Two of the incendiaries were promptly contained, but the third had lodged itself in a stone ornamentation near the roof, and was proving difficult to get at. Auxiliary Fire Service members arrived on the stairwell with a hose, but for a while the water source was blocked. When the water finally began to flow, the stairs were transformed into what Dr Williams later described as a 'Niagara'. Clearly it was time for non-firefighters to vacate the Victoria building.

The Grosvenor Hotel had an air-raid shelter as part of its extensive basement. Despite the overcrowded conditions down there, the dull thunder of the heavier-calibre bombs and the earthquake-like shudder as time after time they hit the city during the twelve-hour raid, the mood generally in the shelter was commendably calm. Dr Williams, a well-known figure locally even when not wearing his church robes, would have been a factor in maintaining this lack

The shell of the Victoria Buildings after the Blitz. St Mary's Gate leads down to Deansgate on the left, and Victoria Street, with the statue of Oliver Cromwell visible at the far end, on the right. *(Greater Manchester Police Museum and Archives)*

of panic. His spectacles and white, receding hair gave the impression of a middle-aged academic, which indeed he was: a qualified physician and surgeon from London University, and with a number of published books to his name. Described as a pleasant and friendly man with a gift for bringing out the best in people, he was also a spry and energetic character, considering he was approaching his sixtieth year, and was renowned for some spirited and well-attended sermons delivered from the pulpit. He was, incidentally, no stranger to real earthquakes, having experienced a couple whilst working at a mission in India during the First World War.

Dr Williams spent much of the remainder of the night in the hotel entrance hall, transfixed by the spectacle of searchlights and fire unfolding across the city sky, and of course concerned about the fate of his beloved cathedral. His written account would later describe the setting as 'a thing of entrancing, shocking, devastating beauty', the cathedral's familiar shape a black silhouette against the backdrop of leaping flames.

One of the last high-explosive bombs to fall before the all-clear at around 6.30 a.m. struck the Lady, Ely and Regimental chapels on the north-east corner of the cathedral. So loud and incessant was the roar from the city-centre inferno that the sound of this detonation was scarcely distinguishable, but its reverberation was felt in the nearby underground shelters.

At the all-clear siren people started to emerge from the many subterranean refuges: besides the Grosvenor's basement, there were around fifteen along Deansgate alone. Between the cathedral and the River Irwell there were the Victoria Arches, converted from old brick landing stages on the river, which were able to house over 1,000 people.

As dawn broke, the air was thick with dust and the stench of smoke from the still burning city, with a golden shower of sparks floating across from The Shambles and Chetham's School, and with the sound of bells of emergency service vehicles intermittently ringing in the few passable streets, Dr Williams, accompanied by an army officer, made the short journey over to his cathedral.

What he saw there must have broken his heart.

The cathedral itself had not caught fire, but the damage was considerable. Every window and door had been blown out, and the lead roof had been lifted clean off by the blast, and then, amazingly, set back down again in place. All the ornaments, chairs and furnishings had been hurled around into heaps. The High Altar was invisible beneath a 10ft-high pile of rubble. The unique medieval woodwork of the choir stalls had been shattered beyond repair. The statue of Sir Humphrey Chetham, by some miracle, though, was virtually untouched. The Lady and Ely chapels on the north-east corner, along with part of the Regimental chapel, had disappeared from the face of the earth. Out of all the cathedrals in Britain it was only Coventry's that had suffered more devastation – and that would have to be completely rebuilt.

Typically, and realising there was nothing he could do here until after the Cleansing and Decontamination Squads had done their bit, Dr Williams thought of his colleagues in the parish. He decided to visit his bishop, who lived a couple of miles away up the hill along Bury New Road, at Bishopscourt in Kersal Dale, over the city boundary in Salford. Without public transport – and with the tramlines mangled by the falling bombs – the trek had to be tackled on foot.

He made his way through the rubble on Victoria Bridge, and passed in front of the Assize Courts on Great Ducie Street. This building was still standing, although it would not survive the attack on the following 1 June, after which only its ornate front facade would remain. Behind it was Strangeways Prison, where the holding cells had been transformed into more air-raid shelters.

The ruins of the cathedral's Lady, Ely, and Regimental chapels, 23 December 1940. (Daily Mail/*Parragon Press*)

By now those inner-city residents rendered homeless by the night's attack would have been making their way to the nearest Rest Centre, such as the one in the converted Assembly Rooms at 109 Cheetham Hill Road. There they would find waiting for them a breakfast and temporary shelter, washing facilities, blankets, mattresses and spare clothes if need be, along with the ubiquitous cup of tea. The Parks Department had loaned deck-chairs, an incongruous but welcome facility for weary legs.

Bury New Road follows the route of the old straight-as-a-dye Roman road from Mamucium to Bremetennacum (Ribchester), but having to keep making detours because of the fires and damage, Dr Williams found that the uphill journey, 2 miles as the crow flies, was proving to be more circuitous than he'd expected. Away to the west smoke was rising from the devastation of Manchester's sister city of Salford. The full appalling damage to Salford and the number of its civilians killed was kept quiet for most of the war for reasons of security and morale. The acrid smell of burning would not have lessened as Dr Williams made his slow way northward along the road above Kersal Dale.

Eventually he reached Bishopscourt, situated on high ground overlooking the great north-south loop of the Irwell. Here he shared a cigarette and a hearty breakfast with his bishop, Guy Warman. The still smouldering chapel roof of Bishopscourt was awaiting atten-tion from the fire service, persuading the dean that the 68-year-old Warman had 'had a night of it' too.

Then Dr Williams retraced his steps, back down Bury New Road to the cathedral. By now a group of people, mainly vergers and mem-bers of the Cleansing Department, had gathered in what was left of the building. The first person that the dean saw, however, was the *City News* reporter, Walter Mulligan, who immediately asked Dr Williams if he could be of assistance in any way. The reply was that yes, if the reporter could somehow send a telegram to the dean's wife in Devon informing her that her husband was unharmed, he would be most grateful. Mulligan did so, later that day, from Blackpool, all commu-nications from and to Manchester having suffered a temporary failure.

Amongst the group of people in the ruins were Hubert Worthington and James Brown. Worthington was the cathedral architect, and Brown from Wilmslow promised to contribute from his stock of good Cheshire oak, stating that 'half a dozen of his best craftsmen were on their way'. Ideas of restoration of the building were even now being set in motion.

Another view of the damage to the north-east corner of the cathedral.
(Greater Manchester Police Museum and Archives)

In dealing with these people, Dr Williams said later that he thought he gave the impression of being 'a bit fey'. This sounds as though he was suffering from an understandable touch of mild shock. Nevertheless his next thought was of Canon Peter Green, Rector of St Philip's. The church was a mile or so to the west, along Chapel Street, so across the Irwell back in Salford. Peter Green, who has a blue plaque to his memory on a wall outside Manchester Cathedral, was in his late sixties, a renowned evangelical writer, and, under the pen name of Artifex, author of a forty-year weekly column in the *Guardian*. He and the dean were staunch and long-time friends.

Deansgate was blocked by a fall of masonry from the Victoria Hotel, and further down the street passage was rendered impossible by platoons of firemen hosing the still burning buildings. So the route taken by Dr Williams was probably via the back streets between Deansgate and the Irwell, until he found a crossable bridge over the river on to Chapel Street.

The way would have been in smouldering ruins. The map of Luftwaffe 'hits' (see Appendix 8) shows a cluster around Salford Central Station, spreading north through Lower Broughton and south towards Ordsall. On that clear night there would have been plenty of features easy to spot from the air and which must have drawn the bombers like a magnet: the sweep of the Irwell, then the westward course of the Ship Canal between the expanse of Trafford Park and the diagonal cuts of Salford Docks; the gathering of railway lines towards Manchester Central Station; the proximity of the mercantile hub of Manchester itself.

Nevertheless St Philip's had been spared, and Dr Williams found Peter Green in good spirits, 'positively exuberant after an all-night session similar to my own. He was like a man walking up to the pavilion carrying his bat after knocking up a century.'

The dean's next thought was of his home, the Deanery in Whalley Range, on Wood Road off Upper Chorlton Road, just 2 miles due south of St Philip's. An easy enough walk in peacetime, but once more there were obstacles to contend with.

With major roads across the Irwell/Ship Canal blocked, Dr Williams eventually found a footbridge which he says he was later unable to rediscover. It seems more than likely that he crossed the waterway by Woden Street Bridge. This was known locally as Mark Addy's Bridge, named after a Salford hero who received the George Cross in Victorian times for rescuing people in difficulties in the

Chapel Street, Salford, the morning after the 22 December bombing.
(Greater Manchester Fire Service Museum)

increasingly polluted river. The bridge is still there, leading to the cobbled street that straddles the Bridgewater Canal, linking Salford's Woden Street with Manchester's Hulme Hall Road. Traditionally the bridge marks the end of the Irwell to the east, and the beginning of the Ship Canal to the west.

So Dr Williams made his way southwards through Stretford, also badly damaged by the night's attack. Chester Road was blocked after a high-explosive bomb had hit the nearby Cornbrook Brewery on Trentham Street, killing ten people in the basement shelter. Gas and water mains had been ruptured.

Whichever route Dr Williams now took, he would have seen evidence of the previous night's raids. High-explosive bombs had badly damaged houses on Henrietta Street, Northumberland Road, King's Road, St John's Road, and Upper Chorlton Road. He would have passed within a block of the ruins of East Union Street Police Station, destroyed the previous night by an aerial mine. Six police officers had been killed, and a vital part of the borough's communications system had been wiped out.

He eventually arrived at the Deanery. No. 60 Wood Road is on the corner with College Road, facing the Lancashire Independent College. It was built in 1899, its original name being Doenberg. Recently converted into flats, the building now bears the name of Cambrian House.

Dr Williams described the Deanery as 'a shambles'. Nonetheless he found a clean enough corner where he changed into fresh clothes before setting out for central Manchester and his cathedral once more.

He was approaching St Peter's Square with its new 'pudding basin' Central Library. The dark red bulk of the Midland Hotel loomed to his left, and Dr Williams suddenly remembered the speech he was due to give to the Luncheon Club, the notes for which were still in his hip pocket. It was five minutes to one, so by a happy chance, he was just in time.

Undeterred by the day's 10-mile walk, after a wash and a quick bite to eat the dean delivered his address to an audience of around seventy, on schedule at 1.30 p.m. This makes for a cheering parable: despite the devastation and upheaval, in many respects it was 'business as usual'.

Although it would take nearly twenty years for the cathedral to be fully restored, enough repairs had been made for a service to be held on Ash Wednesday, 20 March 1941. Dr Williams was back after a leave of absence in Buxton. He would spend the next seven years in tirelessly supervising the cathedral's resurrection, until his retirement in 1948. By then the City of Manchester would be well into its peacetime programme of rebuilding, restoration, and healing of the scars of the Blitz.

The immediate future, however, was much less benign. As night fell over the city on that Monday, 23 December 1940, on the airfields of northern France squadrons of bomb-laden Heinkels and Junkers were already preparing for take-off, destination north-west England.

Manchester's Christmas Blitz was only half over.

SE PUTTIN
RESPIRA

1. Hold you
(To inhale gas m
2. Hold mask
face, thumbs ins
3. Thrust chin w
into mask. Pull
far over head as
go. 4. Run fing
face-piece taking c
straps are not

ITS

ugly
chin.
ad-
the
To
oft,
ue
nd
or

*Arrows indicate points needi
particular attention*

PIRATOR

YOUR EYES, NOSE,
INST ALL WAR GASE
R RESPIRATOR
EFFICIENT

T ONCE PUT ON
ET UNDER COVER

S., Ltd. 428.   34—9999

TWO

'FOREWARNED IS FOREARMED': THE GATHERING STORM

• THE PAPER WAR •
• HITLER'S OPENING SHOTS •
• BUILD-UP TO THE BLITZ •
• THE WORK OF THE
EMERGENCY COMMITTEE •
• SHELTERS, SOFAS AND STAIRCASES •
• REST CENTRES •
• ATTACKS IN JULY – AUGUST 1940 •

In September 1939 the German tanks had rolled into Poland, and Britain's PM Neville Chamberlain, in announcing the declaration of war on the 3rd of the month, had as much as admitted that he had been hoodwinked by Hitler. 'Peace in our time' had become a bad joke.

After Dunkirk there was a pause in Hitler's *blitzkrieg* conquests. Poland, the Low Countries and France had fallen with staggering speed. In the summer of 1940 Hitler was convinced that Britain, standing alone, its army in disarray and minus most of its military land equipment left behind in France, would soon capitulate. As German Air Minister

Hermann Göring put it after France's surrender in June: 'My Luftwaffe is invincible … And so now we turn to England. How long will this one last – two, three weeks?'

The global events have been documented many times elsewhere. What concerns us here is the ever more involved role of Manchester in the progression of events.

For a while it was a war fought almost literally on paper. Of interest here is the Nazi High Command publication *German Invasion Plans for the British Isles*. This consisted of three portfolios, in which the geography, weather, transport and industries of the British Isles are presented with military evaluations. Then each area is given a closer scrutiny. It has this to say about Manchester and its surrounding areas:

> Manchester is the prototypical example of an old English industrial town with an extensive belt of slums that presents a serious problem. The unpleasant consequences of the post-war crisis have brought about a partial transition to modern light industry and armament production …
>
> **Troop movements** in the industrial area are partly helped by the density of the road network, but partly hindered by the many factory buildings and settlements.
>
> The rich agricultural lowlands will be able to make a sizeable contribution to **provisions** for a unit.

And of the Ship Canal:

> The **Manchester Ship Canal** from Liverpool to Manchester is the only canal to have been improved into a modern shipping lane. It alone carries almost half of all internal shipping.

One portfolio contains some 130 maps showing potential targets, those of Mancunian relevance being:

> Salford Electrical, electrical goods production
> Salford Station in western Manchester
> Gas works in western Manchester
> Copper works on the River Irwell in the Lower Broughton part of Salford
> Manchester General Post Office

A much more detailed map of Luftwaffe targets is given in Appendix 6.

In other words, Manchester – and by implication, Trafford Park and Salford Docks – was prominent on the Luftwaffe hit list.

As a mark of how high the German confidence was in a relatively straightforward victory, samples from a list of 'important phrases' given in an appendix to the *German Invasion Plans for the British Isles* are illuminating:

Wie heisst diese Stadt?	What is the name of this town?
Wohin führt dieser Weg?	Where does this way lead?
Wo ist das nächste Postamt?	Where is the next Post Office?
Wo können wir schlafen?	Where can we sleep?
Wo kann ich etwas zu essen bekommen?	Where can I get something to eat?

This makes an interesting comparison with a parallel list – 'HERE'S HOW TO GET YOUR NAZI' – published in the *Manchester Evening Chronicle* on 3 July 1940:

SURRENDER	*Ergeben*
DROP THAT GUN	*Waffen ablegen*
KEEP WALKING	*Vorwärts ohne halten*
PUT YOUR HANDS UP	*Hände hoch*
OR I'LL FIRE THIS GUN	*Sonst schiesse ich*

The list had been proposed by a Mr E. Wilson of Didsbury, and it was suggested that it would be 'of particular use to members of the LDV' (soon to be renamed the Home Guard).

This was, of course, the unofficial stance. The official one was given in the leaflet, delivered in June 1940 to every household in the UK, entitled 'If the Invader Comes – What to Do and How to Do It'. The gist of the instructions was 'stay put, don't spread rumours, and don't co-operate with the enemy'. One piece of advice was to make petrol unavailable, or to disable your own car so the invaders couldn't use it. A correspondent to the *Manchester Evening News* (20 June 1940) was more specific:

Perhaps these notes will be of use:

Sugar: this substance does not discolour petrol, but
                plays havoc with an engine if put in the tank in a
                good quantity

Sand:	dreadful stuff, causing blocked carburettor jet. Makes petrol useless
Common soda:	similar to sugar
Treacle:	prevents engine starting and means complete tank removal

In different ways, both sides were gearing themselves up for an invasion.

For the time being Hitler himself was at least going through the motions of keeping his patience. His two-hour-long speech purporting to seek an armistice with Britain was delivered to the Reichstag on 19 July, and a leaflet with the English translation of that speech was dropped in bundles over England in the first week of August.

Hitler's turgid self-justification, via a catalogue of half-truths, may have gone down well at the Reichstag (who was going to say him nay in any case?) but the unabridged text of the translation was never going to find much sympathy in England. Had Hitler overestimated the catalytic effect of the supposed British class conflict, mistakenly relying on his self-image of populist hero?

The leaflet was entitled 'Hitler's Last Appeal to Reason', and although superficially seeming to be just that, the iron fist can still be plainly discerned within the diplomat's kid glove:

> In this hour I feel it to be my duty before my own conscience to appeal once more to reason and common sense in Great Britain as much as elsewhere. I consider myself in a position to make this appeal, since I am not the vanquished begging favours, but the victor speaking in the name of reason …
>
> I do realise that this struggle, if it continues, can end only with the complete annihilation of one or other of the two adversaries. Mr. Churchill may believe this will be Germany. I know that it will be Britain.

The first recipient of the leaflet drop in the Manchester area, so the story goes, was a police constable at Castle Irwell in Salford on 8 August. Unfortunately the officer of the law was struck on the head by an unopened bundle. His helmet prevented any injury, and one may suppose that such an introduction to the Führer's verbiage significantly reduced his enthusiasm for the contents of the package.

Did any member of the public actually read the transcript all the way through? Anecdotal reactions included: the housewife who, fearing germ warfare, sprayed the leaflet with disinfectant; the London

ARP warden who had a photo taken of him pretending to read it, a broad grin giving the game away; tales of Manchester and Salford youngsters who sold the leaflets to collectors for a couple of pence a shot: the official version was that they donated the money raised towards the purchase of war bonds, but one suspects that this may not have been the unvarnished truth. Most of the sheets were picked up by the police and destroyed.

The *Manchester Evening News* published two reports on the leaflet's fate up and down the country. One man charged people a penny to look at his copy, which he had bought for *2d* (1p) one night in a pub. Then he raffled it, and spent the proceeds on 250 cigarettes which he distributed among the local soldiers. Early one morning two Midlands postmen collected leaflets from back gardens and fields, selling them and raising *25s* (£1.25) for war charities.

General public response to the 'Last Appeal to Reason' seems to have run the gamut from anger to amusement to indifference. Or to quote a spontaneous, uncensored comment from Sefton Delmer of the BBC:

> Herr Hitler, you have on occasion in the past consulted me as to the mood of the British public. So permit me to render your Excellency this little service once again tonight. Let me tell you what we here in Britain think of this appeal of yours and what you are pleased to call our reason and common sense. Herr Führer and Reichskanzler, we hurl it right back at you, right in your evil smelling teeth.

This was, of course, again a personal, unofficial reaction (and it caused some unease in BBC's corridors of power) but it captured the people's mood.

All this, coupled with Churchill's 'fight on the beaches' speech of 4 June, made it plain by now that Britain's assumed capitulation was never going to happen. The original schedule for the Nazi invasion – code-named *Operation Sea Lion* – was for September 1940. Then after the invaders' setback in the Battle of Britain, in which air superiority was denied them, *Sea Lion* was postponed: as it turned out, indefinitely.

Manchester was using the few months' grace – its false calm later to be dubbed the 'Phoney War' – constructively.

A workable Civil Defence Scheme had been in existence in the city, on paper at least, since October 1936. Elsewhere in the country, only three other authorities had kept pace with Manchester: Coventry, Newcastle-on-Tyne, and Leeds. One event in the Manchester Defence Scheme was a trial blackout on 31 March 1939. Just after midnight 800 square miles around the city were plunged into an experimental darkness, simulating war conditions. Some 3,000 observers – including three in the Town Hall bell tower – recorded reactions, and concluded that it was 'on the whole, a complete success'. RAF planes were supposed to have flown overhead to add to the observations, but adverse weather conditions prevented it. In April 1939 the Salford ARP, under the supervision of the Chief Constable of Manchester, staged a mock air attack and air-raid drill. Fireworks and the demolition of a building added to the verisimilitude.

Later on it was the work of the council's Emergency Committee that formed the basis of the city's preparation for the Blitz. The fact that Manchester emerged bloodied but unbowed from the widespread devastation that was to follow, the number of deaths and injuries minimised, ready and able to start the healing and restoration process, was fundamentally down to the clear, comprehensive thinking and decision-making of this small group of men.

These days the word 'committee' may suggest a lumbering entity hampered by bureaucracy and personal issues. This was certainly not true of this one. With the threat of annihilation looming on the horizon, focus was assured. Firstly the numbers attending were low: usually between three and six. Secondly lines of communication between the Town Hall and police, fire and rescue services and whichever public or private companies were involved, were swift and clear. Thirdly the elected chairman, Alderman Sir Robert Noton Barclay, was the perfect man for the job. One of the last great philanthropists, Sir Robert, former Lord Mayor and director of the Ship Canal Company, had been known to buy up scenic Lake District land and donate it to the National Trust. He was now approaching 70 years of age, and his experience, clarity of thought, and natural public-spiritedness (plus a no-nonsense approach to red tape) made him the ideal candidate.

As an indication of the painstaking attention to detail which was the hallmark of the wartime Manchester Emergency Committee, here is a list of selected items from the agenda of just one meeting on 18 October 1940:

Provision of shelter accommodation

Enlargement and improvement of Anderson shelters

St Philip's C. of E. School, Hulme: proposed children's shelter

Salvage of property, storage of furniture, from untenantable houses

Inspection of houses rendered dangerous by air raids

Purchase of heavy boots and eyeshields

Provision of bunks for air-raid shelters

Rescue service – additional equipment (e.g. leather gloves)

Temporary mortuary service

Accommodation and emergency feeding for persons rendered homeless

Government coal stocking scheme

Auxiliary fire service – conversion of vehicles

Provision of community feeding centres

Mobile canteens for auxiliary fire service members

'Accommodation and emergency feeding for persons rendered home-less' refers to the Rest Centres: converted halls, churches or school buildings such as the one on Cheetham Hill Road mentioned in the previous chapter. They were staffed mostly by relays of workers from the Women's Voluntary Service: unpaid and largely unsung, these hard-working ladies were to make an invaluable contribution to Manchester's defence. There were over sixty Rest Centres in the City of Manchester, situated so that there was no more than 2 miles between them. They were usually stocked with chests of tea, sacks of sugar, tinned food and rudimentary meals, access to plenty of hot water, and if need be, clothing, sheets and mattresses. Local parks supplied deckchairs. Later additions were babies' bottles and feed, and soap and towels. Food was supplied by the following:

Manchester and Salford CWS	51 Downing St, Ardwick
Duncan and Fosters	102 York St, C-on-M
Smallmans	Heald Grove, Rusholme
Agars	30 Wilbraham Rd, Fallowfield
Robinson and Smith	Bank St, Levenshulme
U.C.P.	Russell St, Levenshulme

A full list of the Rest Centres in Manchester, Salford and Stretford, including the ones that were used just once or twice during the periods of heaviest bombardment, is given in Appendices 4, 5 and 7.

Separate from these were the Communal Food Centres, usually set up in a school or a mobile canteen, often a converted van. Whereas the food and refreshment was free to the homeless in the Rest Centres – the council had seven days in which to settle accounts with the caterers – the Food Centres were expected to be run as an on-site business concern. A typical price list would be:

½ pint mug of soup	1*d* [one old penny]
1 mug of tea	1*d*
½ pint of stew	4*d*
Biscuits with margarine	3 for 1*d*
Bread and margarine	3 slices for 1*d*
Rice pudding	2*d*
Substantial meat and veg dish	6*d*

(Twelve old pence, or a shilling, were equal to 5p)

Generally, everything seems to have been thought of, down to protective kneepads for rescuers, ARP armlets (£18 4*s* 7*d* per 500), and readily available emergency or 'iron' rations for rescuers or firefighters called away to another authority. These rations were supplied in cartons by the Co-operative Wholesale Society (CWS) – whose praises we will have reason to sing later – and consisted of:

> 1 tin of steak and kidney pudding
> 1lb Army Biscuits
> 1oz tea
> 4oz sugar
> 1 tin milk
> ½lb slab cake
> ½lb digestive biscuits
> 1 bar milk chocolate

Total cost: 3*s* 2½*d* [16p]

There was to be a compensation fund for civilians who'd had clothing or property damaged in the course of rescue service.

There was even a memo concerning the Belle Vue Zoo animals deemed dangerous if freed from their cages by a bomb. Chief

Constable Maxwell, fearful of carnivorous beasts roaming the streets of Gorton and Longsight, suggested shooting them, which horrified the zoo manager. The hit list included thirteen lions, six tigers, two leopards, one cheetah and assorted bears. The manager argued that the cages were so strong that only a direct hit would create enough damage to free the animals, and a direct hit would probably kill them anyway. Eventually a compromise was reached: the zookeepers were allowed to carry firearms, for use in case of a break-out. Happily no bombs hit the zoo. (For another story concerning exotic animals on Hyde Road during the Blitz, see Chapter Three.)

Zookeepers were not the only ones to receive this special privilege of bearing arms. For a short time, whilst there was the daily fear of Nazi paratroopers landing, Manchester police constables on the beat carried a rifle and five rounds of ammunition. The police force was augmented by the designation of part-time special constables, whose remit was to assist the ARP wardens during air raids.

Blackout regulations came into force even before war was declared. From sundown on Friday, 1 September 1939 it was mandatory to cover all interior domestic lights with thick blackout curtains, and street lamps would not be lit again for another five years. One lad who grew up during the war remembers being unaware of what lamp-posts were for, assuming they were purely decorative! Car headlamps had to be covered with newspaper, and there was a universal speed limit of 20mph. Pedestrians were allowed to carry small torches with a no. 8 battery and with the top part of the light covered.

A major issue early on in the preparations was the distribution of gas masks. With memories of the horrors of mustard gas in the First World War trenches still looming in the collective memory, and the conviction being that the warmongering Hun would try the same underhand tactic in any forthcoming conflict, gas masks were at first a mandatory possession of every man, woman and child in Britain. There was a Mickey Mouse-style mask for younger children, and school pupils had classes in how to put them on and use them. Decontamination centres were created at Harpurhey, Trafford and Levenshulme Baths. It was only when it became clear that the enemy was not going to stoop so low that the gas mask was no longer of top priority. The use of toxic gas contravened Hitler's expressed idea of 'clean' warfare, in which there was a simple head-to-head struggle of technology and will, without any deceit or unfair advantage. (This was why, later in

PRACTISE PUTTING ON YOUR RESPIRATOR

1. Hold your breath. (*To inhale gas may be fatal.*) 2. Hold mask in front of face, thumbs inside straps. 3. Thrust chin well forward into mask. Pull straps as far over head as they will go. 4. Run finger round face-piece taking care head-straps are not twisted.

MAKE SURE IT FITS

See that the rubber fits snugly at sides of jaw and under chin. The head-straps should be adjusted so that they hold the mask firmly on the face. To test for fit, hold a piece of soft, flat rubber or of soft tissue paper to end of mask and breathe in. The rubber or paper should stick.

Arrows indicate points needing particular attention

YOUR RESPIRATOR

COMPLETELY PROTECTS YOUR EYES, NOSE, THROAT AND LUNGS AGAINST ALL WAR GASES

ALWAYS KEEP YOUR RESPIRATOR SAFE, CLEAN AND EFFICIENT

IF YOU SUSPECT GAS, AT ONCE PUT ON YOUR RESPIRATOR AND GET UNDER COVER

F/48. (1167/1327.) Wt. 1633. 200M. 8/42. A., P. & S., Ltd. 428.

34—9999

(Ministry of Information)

the war, the hit-and-run guerrilla tactics employed by the partisans of former Yugoslavia enraged Hitler so. Sniping from hidden positions and strategic retreats when faced with superior numbers just wasn't proper warfare. How the Führer squared this idea of fairness with what was going on in the ghettoes and the 'special treatment' camps in the east is anybody's guess.) There was also, of course, the German fear of Allied retaliation with a similar sort of gas attack.

In any case, preparations for a gas attack were thorough. Gas mask drills became routine. There was a special signal for gas: a loud rattle, as opposed to the undulating wail of the siren for a bomber raid. A Salford resident at the time, Brian Seymour, remembers a board fixed on the outside wall of a house at the end of his street. The board was about 2ft square, and of a 'sort of yellowish-green colour'. Underneath was a notice which said that if the colour was seen to change, it meant that there was mustard gas about, and the police should be informed.

Once the enemy's intentions became clear, however, the number of people carrying gas masks, since this was not enforceable by law, dwindled rapidly. By mid-1940 the mask case was quite often being used as a handy lunch box.

Aside from gas masks, the most wide-ranging task undertaken by the Emergency Committee, after organising the mass evacuation of children in September 1939, was the supervision of the distribution and building of air-raid shelters. Most people had a choice of three: the communal place of safety, the Anderson, or the Morrison.

Households with a garden or back yard were given an Anderson shelter by the government: a total of 2,250,000 by October 1939. However, after this date, if your weekly income was higher than £5 (equivalent to around £230 in 2015 money) you had to fork out for your own (which cost from £6 14s – around £320 nowadays). It came with assembly instructions and involved digging a hole in the garden, creating a subterranean floor (ideally waterproof) out of duckboards, erecting the walls and roof of corrugated steel, and piling sandbags and compacted soil on the roof to create an 'igloo' effect.

Equipping and furnishing the refuge was down to the homeowner. It was a surprisingly robust construction, and could survive just about anything short of a direct hit. Initially intended to accommodate people for a short-lived daylight attack, it was only when the night-long bombing sessions were seen to be the Luftwaffe norm that the shortcomings of the Anderson shelter became clear. It was damp, smelly,

Originally intended as a refuge during short raids, the Anderson shelter is shown here to accommodate a family of seven. *(Ministry of Information/ Internet archive)*

cramped and – since it was gasproof – the unventilated conditions were uncomfortable, unhealthy, and on one occasion, lethal. In Southsea, a man fell asleep in his shelter and was asphyxiated by his heater lamp.

After March 1941 those who preferred to stay indoors, and who had the wherewithal and no cellar, often opted for the Morrison shelter, named after Home Secretary Herbert Morrison. Another do-it-yourself job, this one consisted of a large oblong box 6ft 6in x 4ft x 2ft 6in (height). The walls were of welded steel mesh, and the 'roof' was steel plate. It came with 359 parts, three tools and instructional diagrams. It could double as a dining table when not in use. One publicity photo shows a couple playing table tennis on it. A 'Morrison' was free to households whose total annual income was less than £400 (about £18,400 at today's values) or otherwise cost £7.

Another alternative might have been the Haldane, but this deep shelter design was rejected by the government (see *Hansard*, 17 June 1940), probably because it used too much concrete for those astringent times. An indignant article penned by inventor Professor J.B.S. Haldane, published in the *Daily Worker*, failed to persuade. This was despite the accepted fact that a direct hit by a 1,000lb high-explosive (H.E.) bomb could easily crash top to bottom through five storeys and create major damage in a basement. It was estimated (and not only by Haldane) that the ideal subterranean refuge would be 60ft below ground and topped off with a 15ft layer of concrete. However, given the time factor (it would have taken around eighteen months to build and equip a Haldane shelter) and the available resources, these specifications were unlikely to be adopted.

Commercially produced indoor places of refuge included the 'Home Guard' and the 'Reliance'. The 'Home Guard', manufactured at the Yew Tree Ironworks in Hollinwood, Oldham, cost £18 (about £850 today) – 'enamelling extra'. It had the shape of a 6ft 6in-high coal bunker which, according to the newspaper advert, 'will have the appearance of an additional piece of furniture'. The 'Reliance' cost £14 17s 6d (£14.87, equivalent to around £700 today) and promised 'protection against blast, debris, splinters' and 'immunity from colds and infection'.

Those without the outdoor space for an Anderson, or the money for a Morrison or other indoor sanctuary, could always avail themselves of the nearest communal place of safety, usually subterranean. There were pros and cons to this. There was certainly a community sentiment engendered in many public shelters, but there were also complaints about anti-social behaviour, which appeared to range from pure high spirits to the illegal. See Chapter Seven for more on shelter shenanigans.

Advice on what to take with you into your sanctuary was given by the *Manchester Evening News*: items included warm clothing, your gas mask, any insurance policies, a family snack parcel, some knitting or a book, and – 'indispensable' – a flask of warm tea.

There were still those reckless souls who preferred to stay put and trust to a sofa or the staircase or under the bed. Not without good cause, in some cases: one family in Englefield Grove in Gorton were sitting on a settee in the living room of their house when the bomb fell. The force of the blast upturned the settee, covering them, and it was this that saved them from the falling masonry of the blitzed house. Others, noticing that in houses already bombed it was the staircase that always seemed to be left standing in the midst of the rubble, decided to huddle under the stairs when a raid started. Still others, usually of the older generation, simply stayed in bed, reasoning fatalistically that if the bomb 'had your name on it', there was nothing you could do about it.

On a more pragmatic note, the Manchester Fire Service had also undergone thorough preparations. An Auxiliary Fire Service (AFS) was initiated: by the beginning of 1939, fifty-five emergency fire stations had been created, over 6,500 volunteers had been asked for, and £18,000 had been set aside by Manchester Council for supplementary equipment – mostly motor or trailer pumps. Many private cars became temporary improvised fire vehicles. Stirrup pumps were available at the cost of £1 each, and there were training films on their use in the event of incendiary bombs, as well as hands-on coaching sessions in the street.

Extra equipment for firefighting and cleansing was held in fourteen District Depots, the furthest south being Sharston Manor. A Town Hall memo from September 1939 indicates the following total estimated supplementary requirements:

Overalls	13,000
Hurricane lamps	200
Izal disinfectant	100 gallons
Refuse bins	42

The industrial estate at Trafford Park had made its own preparations for war. Landmarks were either disguised or got rid of: sawdust was sprinkled on the Bridgewater Canal, and the Metrovicks water tower (rightly considered too obvious a target for the bombers) was demolished, leaving a stump which was used as a platform for an anti-aircraft gun. Patches of open ground were studded with piles of kerbstones to deter the landing of enemy aircraft. Factory roofs were painted green to make them look like fields, a ploy which was also used by Barton Power Station further west, A.V. Roe in Newton Heath, and Hans Renold in Burnage, amongst others.

In Trafford Park, as in some rural and urban areas, road and directional signs were removed, along with names of companies that would give orientation clues to any invader. The huge concrete cellars of Metropolitan-Vickers Electrical Co. Ltd, commonly known as Metrovicks, proved most useful as air-raid shelters, and more were dug and fully equipped.

The extensive preparations for war undertaken by the Trafford Park Industrial Estate, the hammering that it sustained in the Blitz, and how it still managed to continue significant production in vital areas, is the subject of a later chapter.

In Manchester, the big firms were making their own preparations too. Typical was the Calico Printers' Association on Oxford Road, who converted their eight basement rooms into refuges for 1,100 employees. One of the rooms became a hospital, with first-aid post, blankets and stretchers.

At the outbreak of war the two largest underground communal places of refuge in central Manchester were in the Victoria Arches mentioned above, and the Manchester and Salford Junction Canal (MSJC) tunnel, from which over a million gallons of water were drained off to render it more or less serviceable. This disused canal branch ran beneath the streets for over 800 yards, from the Irwell in the west, under Grape Street (until recently the site of the Quay Street Granada TV Studios) and Camp Street, below Deansgate as far as Lower Mosley Street. The eastern end under Central Station was reserved for the use of employees of Copley-Smith & Sons. This section had electric lighting, plug sockets for radio, and an emergency store of food. Conditions generally in the tunnel, however, were poor, although the first two to three years of war were to see dramatic improvements (see Chapter Seven).

Important buildings such the Town Hall and the Shipping Office on Cockspur Street were surrounded by sandbags. There were two supposedly top-secret underground control centres, both set deep and reinforced with concrete: the one in charge of Manchester was under the Town Hall, and the North West Control Centre was underneath Arkwright House – now a swish bar and some offices – in Parsonage Gardens. This latter hub was responsible for the defence and welfare of over 7 million people, from the Scottish borders to the Derbyshire Peak District. Keith Warrender gives a detailed description of wartime personnel and resources deployed in this extensive cellar in his fascinating book *Below Manchester* (see Bibliography).

Personal protection, for those whose duties took them into the open air, was provided by steel helmets, or 'tin hats' as they were universally known. These cost 5s 6d (27p) each, but were very hard to get hold of before they appeared on the Emergency Committee agenda in 1941. Before that, Mancunian ingenuity (or recklessness) was sometimes brought into play:

> He [speaker's father] was acting stage manager at The Palace [Theatre] … he couldn't get a tin hat anywhere. So what he used to do, he used to get … his jacket and his raincoat and something else. And he used to make a bundle of it and tie it on his head … with his scarf. And he used to go home like that.
>
> And my gran said to him, 'I'll bet you look a bugger walking down Ashton Old Road like that.' And he says, 'Well if it hits me anywhere else I stand a chance, but if it knocks my bloody head off – I've had it!' So that was his protection on his head, walking round with a big bundle.
>
> Charlie Waterfield (*North West Sound Archive*)

On 20 June Mancunians underwent an air-raid practice run. The siren drill may have been a source of irritation or even indifference in some areas at the time, but it would ultimately help focus attention on the practicalities of shelter use. Hospitals and first-aid posts were praised for their swift and efficient reactions to the 'raiders alert' siren – a warbling note 'like a singer running up and down the scale'. However, almost incredibly, there were reports of Manchester residents not taking the drill too seriously, some of them sitting on doorsteps and looking with curiosity up at the summer sky, and casually lighting the odd forbidden cigarette. A strongly worded article in that night's *Manchester Evening News* hoped to rectify matters before the real bombs fell. They would not have long to wait.

The first Luftwaffe bomb to be dropped on the British Isles during the Second World War had been on the Orkney island of Hoy in October 1939.

The target was no doubt the Lyness/Scapa Flow Naval Base and the nearby oil storage tanks. It was also a test of distance flown, weather conditions, navigation – in short, all the logistics of an aerial bombing expedition over the far north of the British Isles. If the Orkneys could be hit and the plane could return safely to a base in Germany without refuelling, an aerial attack on the whole of mainland Britain could be easily accomplished.

The following year, on 16 March, it was a resident of the Bridge of Waithe on the Orkney mainland who was the first British civilian casualty of the war.

After the French capitulation three months later, and the subsequent preparation of dozens of new airfields in Normandy, Picardy and the Pas de Calais, the Luftwaffe was ready for the invasion. However, the repulse in the Battle of Britain forced Hitler to put the land attack on hold. Also relevant, as his generals pointed out to him, was the lack of amphibious craft with which to land tanks on the narrow south-east England beaches. Another phase in the war was approaching.

At the end of July, ten days before the 'Last Appeal to Reason' leaflets were dropped, the first H.E. bombs fell on Salford, on the corner of Trafford Road and Ordsall Lane. A transport time-keeping office was damaged, but there were no casualties. The intention seems to have been an intimidatory prelude to the leaflets' attempt to persuade. As we have seen, neither had much effect.

The sporadic raids became more continuous. High-explosive bombs were dropped on Baguley and Brooklands on the night of 28–29 August. Again there were no casualties, as most fell harmlessly on fields and gardens. The same night Worsley was hit, and some people were injured. Worst affected was Altrincham, where a petrol store caught fire and many houses were damaged.

The next night gave some indication of how bad it was going to get. Hulme, Moss Side, Rusholme and Platt Fields received a barrage of nine HE bombs. To make matters worse, the first of these was dropped on Hulme some twenty minutes *before* the warning siren sounded. Six people were killed, including a family of four living at 47 Peel Street. A Private McCormick was home on leave and drinking with his wife in a nearby pub when he heard the bomb fall. Rushing back home, he found Peel Street in ruins. Spotting a child's limb in the rubble and immediately thinking of his own children, he started to clear a way with his bare hands. The fire brigade arrived and finished the task, and they discovered that the child was John Andrews, one of the family from No. 47. Private McCormick's own children were safe, having gone to visit neighbours.

On 30 August it was Salford's turn again: houses and business premises were hit on Granville Street and Chorley Road.

Elsewhere in England raids were being intensified. Although much worse was to come, throughout August, London, Birmingham, Coventry and Liverpool had been successfully targeted by German bombers. Ominously, Göring referred to these sorties as 'armed reconnaissances'.

In confirmation of this, on the same day as the second attack on Salford, the German News Bureau gave a clear indication of what was to follow: 'The attacks of our Luftwaffe are only a prelude. The decisive blow is about to fall.'

THREE

'THE BOMBER WILL ALWAYS GET THROUGH': KNOW THE ENEMY

- CIVILIANS AS TARGETS -
- HEINKELS AND JUNKERS -
- LUFTWAFFE GUIDANCE SYSTEMS AND THE MOW COP JAMMER -
- TYPES OF BOMB -
- TOWARDS TOTAL WAR -
- ATTACKS SEPTEMBER – MID-DECEMBER 1940 -

When the detonating bombs ripped through the densely populated residential areas of Hulme, Stretford, Ordsall, Lower Broughton, Ancoats and Chorlton-on-Medlock, survivors could be forgiven for concluding that it was Luftwaffe policy to target non-combatants. Pure terror bombing, however, was rarely the expressed theoretical aim of either side, at least initially, even though ultimately, in practice, it certainly turned out that way.

From the mid-thirties onward the possibility of civilian casualties in a forthcoming war had been considered, and prepared for by legal statute. We have seen the forethought and preparation for such a conflict in Manchester. Other English cities copied the Manchester plan, so it was clear that the general feeling was that non-combatants away from the war front would no longer have a guaranteed safety in the forthcoming conflict. There were a number of reasons for this.

An influential book, *The Command of the Air*, had been required reading for air force strategists in Germany and the USA (but not, perhaps significantly, in Britain) throughout the decade. Its author, General Giulio Douhet of the Italian Air Force, was a firm believer that intensive and indiscriminate aerial bombardment of an enemy city would bring about either social and infrastructural collapse or the uprising of the city's people against their leaders (as with the Paris Commune of 1870). In other words, according to Douhet, in that pre-atomic age the dropping of airborne bombs could win a war by sheer scale of destruction, whatever the targets.

The resistance and stubborn cohesion of the English cities – not least Manchester – during the Second World War helped to disprove Douhet's theories. The war in Europe was eventually won by a combination of air power and a massive land invasion. (So it could be argued that 'Bomber' Harris's 1945 saturation bombing of Dresden and other German cities was strategically pointless as well as morally reprehensible.)

Douhet's book had been published in 1920, and its author had died in 1930. By the outbreak of the Second World War, the ideas expressed in *The Command of the Air* were already looking to be from an earlier aeronautical age. The destruction of the Basque town of Guernica by German and Italian planes in 1937, in which according to some estimates over 1,000 civilians were killed, was an atrocity condemned by most of the free world. The attack, however, failed to put an end to the town's Assembly, and symbolically the community's oak tree of liberty remained unharmed after the raid.

Luftwaffe commander-in-chief Hermann Göring was sceptical about the value of indiscriminate terror bombing, preferring to hit industrial and military installations, transport hubs, and cultural centres. When Hitler, in one of his famous rages, ordered widespread attacks across London following the RAF's destruction of the port of Lübeck in 1942, Göring privately ignored the directive. He failed to see the military value of targeting civilians.

Also, the reader is referred to the Luftwaffe reconnaissance maps of Manchester (Appendix 6). It is only the industrial, chemical and transport centres that are numbered and highlighted. The adjoining residential suburbs are ignored as military targets.

But the question remains: in that case, why were there so many civilian casualties, and why were there so many residential areas hit, during the Manchester Blitz? (Or as one Stretford gentleman was to put it, several years later: 'Hitler? He couldn't hit a cow's arse with a banjo.') Whether due to inaccuracy or a deliberate terror policy, the answer will, of course, apply to other British cities under attack.

Firstly, it will be useful to look at the war technology available to the Luftwaffe in 1940.

The aeroplanes used by the German air force in the Manchester Blitz were almost exclusively Heinkels and Junkers. The Heinkel 111 had been developed for over six years: even before Hitler's rearmament programme, the plane's long-distance capabilities had been tested and improved under the guise of a civilian and cargo transport vehicle. A range of almost 750 miles (1,250km), top speed of 270mph (410km/h) and a maximum freight load capacity of 4,000lb, had all the capabilities of a potential bomber.

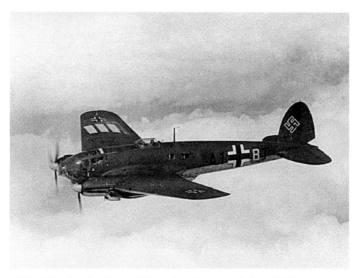

A Heinkel 111 bomber. This model was phased out towards the end of the war, replaced by the Junkers 88. *(Deutsches Bundesarchiv)*

The Heinkel 111, still with civilian markings, had made a significant contribution to the Luftwaffe's compilation of aerial reconnaissance photos in the years immediately preceding the Second World War. Under the guise of goodwill flights – along with the Dornier 17 and the airship *Hindenburg*'s tour of southern England in 1936 – major industrial and economic hubs and transport details were visually recorded for future use. Then, adding insult to covert injury, to help defray the cost of the enterprise, souvenir copies of the photographs were sold to the British populace! Surprisingly, this was the only aerial survey of the British Isles until the RAF repeated the process in 1947.

For war purposes, the Heinkel had a five-man crew: the pilot, the navigator/captain, who was also the crew member who decided at which point the bombs would be dropped; the in-flight engineer, the radio operator, and the gunner. This last had a choice of six gun placements, but was usually positioned in a smaller cockpit situated below the pilot and navigator, or in the belly of the plane. (The question of whether British civilians and firefighters were deliberately machine-gunned will be addressed later.)

The Heinkel, however, was being phased out at the time of the Manchester Blitz. Deemed comparatively slow and poorly armed against land or air attack, it was gradually to be replaced by the more modern Junkers 88. Introduced in 1939, this was a more versatile

A Junkers 88, the bomber responsible for over half the Manchester raids.
(Deutsches Bundesarchiv)

machine with a bomb weight capacity of up to 3,100lb (1,400kg), maximum speed of 320mph (510km/h), and a range of 1,430 miles (2,430km). The versatility included gunner options, most significant of which was the possibility of carrying an MGFF auto-cannon, which fired high-explosive mine shells at the rate of 520 rounds per minute.

A succession of guidance systems was used to help bombers pin-point targets. First there was the *Knickebein* ('crooked leg') which depended on the intersection of two radio beams trained on the target from different sources. For the North of England, one source was in Kleve (as in Anne of Cleves), near the border with the Netherlands, and on the same latitude as Luton. The other was in Bredstedt in the north of Germany close to the Danish border, roughly 400 miles due east of Middlesbrough across the North Sea. One source sent Morse dashes, the other Morse dots, and when the two signals coincided, the pilot knew that the target had been reached. The French towns of Cherbourg and Calais served the same purpose for southern England.

When *Knickebein* was successfully scrambled by the RAF – partly due to the Bletchley Park decoding of an intercepted Luftwaffe mes-sage, partly due to the expertise of Manchester University-based physicist Professor Douglas Hartree – the Germans responded with the more sophisticated *X-Gerät* guidance system. It was the code name Wotan which led to the RAF managing to jam this device too: Wotan (Odin) was the one-eyed Norse god, and this monocular fea-ture led the RAF interceptors to deduce that this guidance method used basically a single beam, crossed by a secondary beam at crucial points in the flight. This turned out to be an accurate assessment: signals were sent when the aircraft was 10km from the target, then 5km, and finally when directly above it, or rather at the optimum release point, allowing for the distance forward the bomb would travel whilst descending. A jammer situated atop Mow Cop hillock in Staffordshire threw the spanner into these particular works.

A modification of *X-Gerät*, which bore the name *Y-Gerät* (or in Nazi code-speak: Wotan 2), was in operation soon after, and it was this one that – theoretically – guided the Luftwaffe over Manchester. *Y-Gerät* again used a single beam, but this time without a cross beam at all. Signals were sent along the main beam to communicate dis-tance travelled, and therefore distance from target. Once again, this was eventually messed with by the RAF countermeasures, to the degree that, so the story goes, one Junkers 88 was misled into landing on an English airfield!

How accurate were these guidance systems when in full working order?

Richard Overy, in his splendidly comprehensive survey *The Bombing War* quotes the following illuminating exchange between a Luftwaffe major and lieutenant, taken from the War Office National Archives recordings. The extract is transcribed from the translation of a secretly bugged conversation between the captured pilots whilst they were being held at Trent Park, north London:

> Major: *Knickebein* is accurate enough for night work, so that I can simply drop the bombs at that moment.
>
> Lieutenant: But if you drop the bombs at that moment, then if you are at a height of 6,000 metres the bomb will drop 1½ kilometres farther in front, won't it? It doesn't drop vertically.
>
> Major: It doesn't make any difference with such targets.
>
> Lieutenant: Well then, it can't be so accurate.
>
> Major: No, good heavens, as I have just said, it is so difficult even to get to the point of intersection …
>
> Lieutenant: Yes, but why don't your bombs fall accurately?
>
> Major: … you are just told to take the centre of the town and you must each find your own targets.
>
> (Quoted in *The Bombing War*, p. 96)

Clearly, these reservations apply only to *Knickebein*, but even with the more sophisticated guidance systems which followed, inaccuracy, and therefore bomb wastage, was a concern of the German Air Ministry: 'Too many bombs have fallen on open ground far away from the target area ordered. *Bemerkungen zum Einsatz der Luftwaffe* [Remarks on the use of the Luftwaffe 11 January 1941].' (Quoted in *The Bombing War*, p. 95.)

For a conurbation such as Manchester, for 'open ground' one may add 'and built-up residential areas'.

There were other reasons for bombing imprecision. Hitler's self-imposed timetable meant that aircrew lost in battle or due to accidents were being replaced by comparative rookies who lacked the practical experience of bombing raids. British weather being famously temperamental, a clear night sky could rarely be guaranteed for the duration of the attack. Moreover, maps used were sometimes out of date.

Also, diverse attempts at camouflage or misdirection were used by the defenders, with varying degrees of success. At Metropolitan-Vickers in Trafford Park, factory roofs were painted green to make them look like fields. The walls of the Mather and Platt factory in Newton Heath were painted to look like terraced houses, and real gardens were planted alongside, to add to the effect. Large fires were lit on the moors or mosses on the periphery of Manchester (code name operation 'Starfish'), in the hope of luring Luftwaffe navigators away from the 'real' fires in the city centre. Elsewhere, use was made of a smoke generator, an ugly contraption that belched out black smoke from a funnel, the aim of which was to create an artificial cloud cover.

The pilots also had to evade anti-aircraft shells, barrage balloons, and searchlights. To be sure, all three could be ignored if the plane flew high enough, but the higher the flight path, the greater the likelihood of inaccurate targeting. Finally, no Luftwaffe plane was allowed to return with anything remaining of the bomb load, so sometimes bombs were dropped anywhere on the way back just to get rid of them.

Unpredictability, of course, increases the terror aspect of bombing. It should be mentioned that the RAF's navigational systems were even more unreliable, and their results even more random, than those of the Luftwaffe. The Nazi propaganda machine made much of German civilian casualties, and this helped to escalate the war to a mind-set which saw non-combatants as fair game, if only for revenge purposes. The German High Command issued the following, as early in the war as June 1940: 'Since May 10th enemy aircraft, mainly British, have continued to attack German towns during the night. Last night four civilians lost their lives. The German Air Force has therefore begun to wreak vengeance on Britain.' (*Manchester Evening News*, 20 June 1940)

September and October 1940 saw a steady increase in raids on Manchester. A full-scale attack would involve an initial dropping of hundreds of incendiary bombs, possibly after parachute flares to defeat the purpose of the blackout. The fires thus started would act as a guide for the next wave of bombers arriving an hour or so later. These would be carrying the high-explosive devices such as the parachute mines, and the nasty *am Ende das Gift*: the oil bomb.

An incendiary or smaller firebomb was a cylinder 14in long, composed of a magnesium casing with a thermite core. Although a single incendiary looks nothing special, it was the sheer number of these

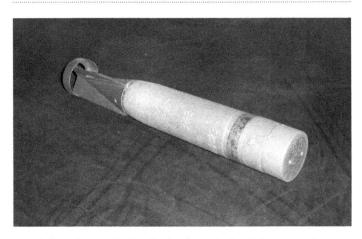

Just 14in long, the incendiary bomb, when dropped in hundreds, was nevertheless difficult to contain if not dealt with immediately. *(Author's collection/Imperial War Museum North)*

devices dropped that created the problem. A plane would typically carry twenty boxes containing thirty-six incendiaries each, so it was possible for literally thousands of these bombs to be dropped in a single raid. The technology was simple: the device was primed during its fall, as the airflow acted on a metal disc which pulled out the pin from the impact fuse. On detonation, the thermite reacted with the magnesium and a small but very bright fire would be ignited. A single such fire, if reached in time, was relatively easy to extinguish: the quick deployment of a stirrup pump or some heavy material would probably do the trick. However, a lot of the incendiaries, since dropped at night, fell on empty office blocks where there was no one on duty to report or combat the flames. And in sufficient numbers and with an inflammable target, they would rapidly escalate into an uncontainable blaze.

The high-explosive bomb, or H.E., was a generic term covering devices ranging between 50 and 1,800kg. A cardboard cylinder attached to the H.E. bomb made a whistling sound as it fell: hence the nickname whistling or screaming bomb. The sole point of this piece of theatre was to unnerve those below. Even dummy H.E. missiles fitted with the tube served an intimidatory purpose, as evacuation of the immediate area had to be undertaken, with a resultant drain on rescue services. The real H.E. bombs – or at least the lighter ones – were

A bomb disposal squad retrieve and defuse a buried 1,000lb bomb on Lilac Lane in Moss Grove, Oldham, after the raid of 12 October 1940. *(Greater Manchester Police Museum and Archives)*

often let fall in a 'stick', or succession of individual drops, one closely following the other. This increased the likelihood of a specific target being hit, although of course with significant collateral damage.

Parachute or aerial mines – often incorrectly called landmines – consisted of a large 8ft-long device. These were carried externally under the wing of the aircraft, in the area closest to the fuselage. Because of their weight (up to 1,000kg) they were usually carried in pairs so as not to unbalance the plane, and dropped in quick succession for the same reason. Each of these devices had the capacity to create widespread devastation.

Another type of bomb dropped by the Luftwaffe was one with a timer that caused a delayed explosion some time after impact. Typically this device would be equipped with a vibrating mechanism which would enable the bomb to burrow to a depth of around 6m, where it would lie dormant before detonating several hours later.

Finally there was the most unpleasant fruit of pre-atomic war technology: the oil bomb. This would arrive silently, again by parachute, which often prompted onlookers to make the fatal mistake of rushing towards them, thinking there was a paratrooper landing. The device was about the size and shape of a dustbin, with a thin metal casing packed with oil and other inflammable material. On impact, caused by the slightest collision with anything solid, the bomb burst and flung out flaming oil and shrapnel for many yards around.

On the night of 31 August a single raider dropped a stick of H.E. bombs along the railway line from Deansgate-Knott Mill Station to Ardwick. Commercial property was damaged, including a warehouse behind the Palace Theatre. The rumour that the Palace had been destroyed with great loss of life had some currency for a while, until proven untrue. A bomb dropped clean through the Fairfield Street railway bridge, and two houses in Lime Street, Ardwick, were destroyed by a direct hit.

Four nights later it was Salford again. The matron of the Old People's Home section of Hope Hospital usually spent the night with her maid sheltering and sleeping under the kitchen annex, but on that particular night, acting on a premonition, she insisted that both of them abandon their usual place of safety. A few minutes after leaving the annex they heard a terrific crash: a bomb had fallen on the kitchen, completely wrecking that wing of the building. The roof of the ward which held the forty-five high-dependency patients had been blown away, but despite this they maintained their dignity. The matron related: 'The eldest patient Susan Shaw, who is 92, was buried under plaster. When we ran to her she was murmuring "God forgive him". We knew who she meant.' There was just one casualty: a 58-year-old who died of shock.

Along Eccles New Road, over in Weaste, that same night saw an oil storage shed at Berry Wiggins oil processing plant hit by an H.E. It took the regular fire brigade, the AFS, and units from other areas three hours to extinguish the blaze. Some of the firefighters had to be treated for burns, and auxiliary fireman Arthur Holt was to die from his injuries a month later.

For the rest of September 1940, with one exception, bombs fell relatively harmlessly on potato fields, golf courses, and sheep. The exception was Irlam on the 9th, where H.E. bombs were dropped on Liverpool Road, and there were several casualties. Thirteen H.E. bombs fell on Heaton Park one week later, but besides leaving several craters in the grounds and on the golf course – and one detonation, which 'seemed to lift the Hall from the ground' according to the gardener's wife – the only damage to property was a single broken window. Fortunately, it was only later in the war that Heaton Park would become a major RAF training centre.

Overall, though, there appeared to be a lull, so much so that a member of the Emergency Committee tempted fate with the (minuted) statement: 'The City has again escaped any damage of national importance.' Well, so far, perhaps.

The 1 October raid left a total of twenty dead, and was proclaimed the 'most serious to date'. An oil drum incendiary was dropped on Moorfield Street, Withington, killing all nine occupants of a domestic surface shelter. Another bomb fell outside the White Lion Hotel, killing an ARP messenger boy on his bicycle. In Fallowfield, two houses on the corner of Walter Street and Sherwood Street were demolished. Three bodies were retrieved from the rubble.

Salford sustained severe damage during the early October raids. Several oil bombs were dropped, and an H.E. passed through the Town Hall roof, exiting to detonate in East Market Street. A man and wife were thrown from their first-floor bedroom into the crater in the street, but miraculously suffered from not much worse than shock and some bruising. Besides the Town Hall building, local shops and houses, and a sewer and water main, were hit. The Trafford Park Industrial Estate was also a target of widespread bombing.

East Market Street, alongside Salford Town Hall, 2 October 1940, after a high-explosive bomb attack. Two of the residents of the terraced housing on the left had a miraculous escape. *(Greater Manchester Fire Service Museum)*

There was a mixed bag of incidents during that 1 October raid. Shops and houses on Yew Tree Avenue in Moss Side were demolished, and rescuers spent hours digging out 12-year-old Laura Price, who had sustained a badly injured arm when a wooden beam fell across her. Her younger brother Stanley was also buried in the debris, and it was he who was proclaimed the hero of the hour, constantly calling out to the rescuers so they knew where to dig. His first question when emerging was on the whereabouts of his parents, but both had been killed in the attack. A total of nineteen perished in Moss Side, Withington, Fallowfield and Longsight.

No wartime narrative would be complete without a touch of the surreal: in a suburban road in Withington, an explosion had been strong enough to lift a car off the ground and deposit it in the first-floor bedroom of a neighbouring house.

Over in Audenshaw, the rubber works was hit, causing a serious fire, but fortunately without casualties.

There were many positive signs amidst the destruction. During the 1 October raids on Ardwick, Special Constable J.H. Fletcher was on duty at 10 p.m. when the siren sounded. Immediately afterwards an incendiary fell on No. 14 Holstein Street, dropping down into the kitchen, where it detonated, close to a gas cooker. Fletcher and his son ran into the kitchen, where they encountered 'a very strong glare, and fragments were being thrown about in all directions'. Whilst his son turned off the gas supply at the house's mains, the special constable successfully put out the fire with sand and a bucket of water.

Round the corner on Franchise Street, a fire had gained considerable hold when Fletcher arrived. Having doused the flames with sand and water, the constable dug out the bomb with a spade, then placed it in a bucket and covered it with wet sand. Nor were Fletcher's heroics over for the night. He ran back to Holstein Street, where at No. 2 a wall had collapsed – without casualties – and a number of people were attempting to put out the fire. Fletcher helped them finish the job. As a result of the night's work his boots were charred and deemed useless for further wear. A grateful police force bought him a new pair out of their funds.

There were other courageous acts recorded by the Emergency Committee minutes. On 7 October three incendiary bombs fell on Rochdale Road gasworks: two in the yard, and one on top of the gasholder. Typically, the two ground-level incendiaries proved easy to deal with, but the one on the roof, being harder to access and because of the proximity to the inflammable gas, was a huge threat. Showing scant regard for his own safety, employee Mr Wilkin climbed to the top of the holder and extinguished the bomb where it was. When he was later offered some recognition of his 'act of gallantry', he refused the honour, remarking that it came under 'the ordinary discharge of our duties', so as far as he was concerned, nothing special.

Four days after this incident an incendiary had set fire to the bedroom floorboards of a house in Bishop Street, Moss Side. The ARP warden arrived with his stirrup pump, which failed to work. Occupier James Yates, aged 56, sorted matters himself by throwing his overcoat on the spreading flames, and along with the warden, jumping up and down on top of it until the flames had gone out. There was no mention of an award for this, but his claim for 30s (£1.50) compensation to replace his damaged overcoat was supported by the chief constable and ultimately granted.

One of the most inspiring stories to emerge from those October raids was what happened on the evening of the first of the month at the Hippodrome Theatre, Ardwick, according to a report in the

Manchester Evening News. Not to be confused with the defunct Hippodrome on Oxford Street, nor with the one on Preston Street, Hulme, this popular theatre, situated on Hyde Road opposite the Apollo cinema-cum-ballroom, was formerly known as the Empire, and had been renamed the Hippodrome some five years before. On the night in question the spectacular musical *Tropical Express*, which featured a baby elephant, some monkeys and some harmless snakes, was showing to a packed house. The air-raid siren went, and the manager appeared on the stage to ask the audience if they wanted the show to go on. As he was speaking, the incendiaries started to fall. One pierced the roof and hit the stage curtain, and the manager dived for safety as the 2-ton curtain fell on to the stage behind him. Despite everything, the audience opted to stay. The elephant was led down by its Senegalese minder to the basement to keep company with the monkeys and snakes, and an anonymous lady played the piano whilst the audience sang songs and 'pieces of burning backcloth fell onto the stage'. According to the report 'scantily-clad' chorus girls formed a human chain to deliver buckets of water to douse the fires. (One has to wonder how much this newspaper story was hyped for the purposes of morale, but there is certainly plenty of evidence elsewhere to support the detail of audiences refusing to budge because of an air raid. They'd paid their money, so they were going to watch the show! See *Manchester at War: The People's Story*, pp. 34 and 40.)

Residential areas now seemed to be targeted: Manchester suburbs hit during the October raids included: Chorlton-cum-Hardy, Didsbury, Northenden, Moss Side, Hulme, Chorlton-on-Medlock, Rusholme, Fallowfield, and Collyhurst. A total of forty civilians were killed during the month's raids. The 10 October raid was described by the *Evening News* as 'the longest and most indiscriminate raid yet'. In the Broughton district of Salford twenty people were sheltering in the basement of the Albert Branch Library on Great Clowes Street when an H.E. bomb fell on the nearby pathway. Of the twenty, only eight received minor injuries, the rest emerged unharmed. A few blocks away in Marshall Street an oil bomb destroyed the blast wall of another shelter, but once again injuries were only minor.

During the raid of the night of 12–13 October two adjoining houses in Lincoln Street, Hulme, were demolished, leaving seven dead. The corner house, No. 23, was only partially damaged, but the family of five, including a babe in arms, were trapped in the cellar, with water from a burst water main rapidly rising. The rescue squad were unwilling to shift any of the debris, for fear of bringing down the remains of the house on the people beneath. There was a narrow gap in the rubble, through which the family were visible. Amongst the watching crowd was John Clarke, a 16-year-old apprentice at Metrovicks in Trafford Park. He was deemed thin enough to fit through the gap, so he took it upon himself to enter the wrecked cellar. He reached the distressed family and managed to persuade the mother to let him take care of the baby, which he handed up through the aperture to the rescue squad. Next the three children were passed through, leaving the mother who was 'a bit broad about the hips'. The problem was solved by tying a rope around her ankles and lifting her out feet first, with John adjusting the angle of exit from below. John concludes the story:

> It took about ten minutes, and I was up in a minute, and got out! Then there's a woman screaming on the other side of the street, Denton Street, saying 'It's a miracle! It's a miracle!' I thought, lovely, I've done a miracle, but she didn't mean that. What she meant was, this was the grandmother of the children who we'd got out, they'd been barefooted and they'd run across all the broken glass and debris on the road, without a mark on their feet. So it was a miracle!

As conditions nationwide worsened, significant contributions were made elsewhere in the country. The massive raid on Coventry on 14 November – the one which set the pattern for future large-scale attacks on cities – brought twelve rescue squads from Manchester.

As Christmas approached, Mancunians could be excused for their cautious optimism. The past few weeks had been relatively calm. The only local incidents worthy of concern had been the stray bomb on Button Lane in Wythenshawe on 18 November, and the destruction of a row of shops in Ancoats on 16 December. In the Wythenshawe incident the four children of the Winter family were putting on their shoes to go to the outside shelter when the bomb hit. The mother, Mrs Sophia Winter, appears to have thrown herself on top of the children in a bid to save them. She succeeded, but was herself killed by falling debris. In Ancoats on 16 December the stick of bombs fell at 9 p.m. at night, the target appearing to be the nearby Oldham Road Goods Station. Twelve people were killed.

Generally, though, in spite of everything, the Mancunian mood remained upbeat. Most shops were open, and the trade was good. The traditional Christmas panto was still up and running: Stanley Holloway was starring in *Robinson Crusoe* at the Palace, and Tommy Trinder ('You lucky people!') was playing Buttons in *Cinderella* at the Opera House. Belle Vue had its circus, and there was a full cinema programme. The 9.30 p.m. pub closing time had been relaxed to 10 p.m., and bus conductors had just agreed to work through black-out alerts, at least earlier in the evening. The newspapers were full of raids on Berlin, Hamburg and other German cities, and reports harped on about Hitler's oil, resources and finances being stretched to the limit. So was the worst over? Anything but. The heaviest hammer was about to fall, and those with ears and eyes open needed no top-secret interception of a radio guidance beam to warn them.

Lord Haw-Haw with his 'Germany calling' radio transmission had helpfully announced in his mocking upper-class voice: 'The Manchester people have bought their turkeys for Christmas, but they won't be cooking them.'

The morning of 22 December dawned clear and bright over the city. The cloudless skies would last for at least twenty-four hours, and the full moon of a week before was still bright enough to aid navigation. It was perfect night-bombing weather.

FOUR

'ONE MASS OF FLAMES': CHRISTMAS BLITZ(1): MANCHESTER

• MANCHESTER 22–24 DECEMBER 1940 •
• TALES FROM THE INFERNO •
• ACTS OF GALLANTRY •

The first incendiary bombs of that early Sunday evening of 22 December fell within a couple of minutes of each other, at around 7 p.m., in two small areas of the city centre: the Princess Street and Town Hall corner of Albert Square, and the vicinity of the cathedral, between the north-east end of Deansgate and Victoria Station. They fulfilled their purpose, as wave after wave of Luftwaffe bombers used the flames as a guide to where to unload the follow-up heavy stuff of aerial mines and high-explosive devices. A ruptured gas main on St Mary's Gate added to the fires, and four hours later the whole cathedral/Corn Exchange area was ablaze. The Royal Exchange building on the corner of Cross Street and Market Street had been hit, as had the Victoria Buildings, Miller Street, Victoria Street, and the Exchange Hotel in Fennel Street.

Looking down Exchange Street and Victoria Street, with the cathedral in the distance. *(Greater Manchester Police Museum and Archives)*

As fire bombs, some in ones and twos, others in clusters of a dozen or more, rained down across the city, the fire and rescue services were hard pressed. It should be remembered that the fire brigade was seriously depleted on that first night of the Blitz, as 300 men and thirty pumps were still in Liverpool, fighting the flames from the previous night's raids. Merseyside had also claimed 120 rescue team members from Manchester, along with 450 vehicles that had been customised for ARP use. Some of the remaining improvised fire vehicles, mostly private cars, unused to the new demands imposed upon them, broke down. Nevertheless the Manchester auxiliaries and what remained of the regulars did a splendid job in the circumstances, holding the fort until the return and increase of manpower and equipment the following day.

Deansgate is on the line of the original roadway between the Mamucium Roman fort and village. Around a mile long and almost dead straight, once the fires had taken hold it proved a visible and easily recognisable reference point for the succeeding Luftwaffe squadrons. Rich in commercial and industrial targets, it was also, westwards towards the River Irwell, a sizeable residential area.

Seventeen-year-old Gerry Ennis was preparing to go out on his voluntary fire-watching duties when he heard a thump of something landing on the roof of his parents' terraced house on Welsh Street. (This used to be off Hardman Street, roughly where the shops and restaurants of The Avenue are now.) He climbed out of the gable window on to the roof, where he saw a live incendiary. He kicked it down into the street, where it eventually burned itself out. From his vantage point he saw the bombs falling: 'All sorts of things – incendiaries and land mines – and places were ablaze.' (*The Manchester Village: Deansgate Remembered*, p. 54.)

Further south, on Duke Street, Kathleen Ward spent the following night in the communal air-raid shelter in the basement of Wellington Mill by the railway viaduct. At just after 9 p.m. a high-explosive device was dropped on the street. There was a loud detonation up above and the shelter lights went out, which created some panic. The next morning the residents emerged to find that Duke Street was a heap of rubble, with few houses left standing.

At the southern end of Deansgate the Knott Mill railway and warehouse hub received a severe mauling on the night of 22–23rd. An early incendiary was followed two hours later by a high-explosive device, then by another just before 2 a.m. Another gas main was fractured, and nine people were rescued from the blazing houses in nearby Riga Street and Owen Street and taken to the Zion Rest Centre on Stretford Road.

On the eastern side of Deansgate, Jackson's Row and St Anne's Square had been hit by a shower of incendiaries, causing extensive damage to shops and business premises.

A Knott Mill warehouse ablaze during the December 1940 Blitz. *(Kemsley Newspapers)*

On Peter Street one of the first H.E. bombs destroyed the iconic Free Trade Hall, which would have celebrated its centenary in 1943. Also hit were commercial buildings in nearby Watson Street and Windmill Street. On the other side of St Peter's Square, on the corner of Oxford Street and Lower Mosley Street, the roof of the Bradford Dyers' Association factory was ablaze. The fire proved difficult to quell, spreading rapidly to nearby buildings. So stretched were the fire services that the officer in charge moved on to other fires, leaving an AFS contingent with a single water pump in an attempt to contain the incident. When the officer returned to the scene some hours later he was surprised to see a sailor on leave deploying the hose. The sailor explained that he'd had an argument with his wife and so preferred to lend his presence to the firefighting!

The most serious concatenation of fires was based on the warehouse blocks around Portland Street and Piccadilly. The building contents were mostly flammable cotton, textiles and paper products, so the blaze rapidly spread into an uncontainable inferno. Eventually it took deliberate detonation of undamaged buildings to create firebreaks. One week after the raid, the incident was officially 'still open' and 'in charge of the Military Authorities'.

A saddening cultural loss from this vicinity was a number of irreplaceable manuscripts and memorabilia of Newton, Dalton and Joule in the Literary and Philosophical Society House at 36 George Street.

Nellie Dones recalls that her father, on fire-watch duty at his workplace, Abraham Haworth's cotton store on Bloom Street, had arranged for his family to spend the night in the air-raid shelter in the warehouse basement rather than stay at home in less well-protected surroundings. Nellie, her mother, grandmother and younger brother bunked down in the shelter, but during the night they were awoken by loud explosions outside. A fireman told them they had to leave, as it was too dangerous to stay there, so the four of them made their way between the burning buildings to the communal surface shelters in Piccadilly. On the way they passed Woolworths with the windows blown out and the goods scattered across the pavement. Nellie recalls that they resisted the temptation to help themselves.

They would have passed by Parker Street, which had been the scene of a tragic occurrence earlier in the night. A five-strong AFS contingent, led by Regular Fireman George Albert, had arrived with a mobile pump to quell one of the first warehouse fires, but before they could start their work a high-explosive bomb killed all six.

A similar incident – but without loss of life – took place on Miller Street, between Shudehill and Corporation Street, where the great hardware premises of Baxendale's was ablaze. The AFS turned up to see that both sides of the street were burning, so a decision had to be made as to which side to deal with first. However, the option was forced on them, as almost immediately another bomb hit Baxendale's, rendering work on that side of the street superfluous.

Employees from the hardware store had been trying to salvage portable goods by piling them in wheelbarrows borrowed from the gardening department, but this attempt at damage limitation had been swiftly curtailed by the fires and collapsing masonry.

The Smithfield Market and surrounding streets were strafed with incendiaries. The market roof and offices were badly damaged, as were several premises in Swan Street and Shudehill. The Hare and Hounds, a popular Shudehill pub, was gutted. The incident was reported closed, but the fires started again early on the 23rd. Other nearby pubs lost were the Bull's Head, which had been Bonnie Prince Charlie's headquarters during his march south, and the Slip Inn, which had featured Chaplin and George Formby in its entertainments evenings. The Falstaff and the Temple Bar (also known as Joe Bennett's) were also destroyed.

North of the cathedral the Strangeways district received a battering. The Woolsack pub/hotel on the corner of Southall Street and Great Ducie Street was demolished. Further along Southall Street the police station had one fatality: PC John Burns. Superintendant F. Hogg and Captain A.F. Horden were dug out of the rubble uninjured, but covered with debris and suffering from shock. Local resident Jenny Johnson was in the Assize Courts' holding cells which had been converted into shelters. She remembers:

> And when this bomb fell, I was seventeen then, I had my dog, Peggy, and she was on a lead, and when the bomb fell, it was like a concussion. The windows broke – they just shattered really because they were sandbagged – and it was an awful experience, just like somebody had hit you on the head, and then of course we were all kids, all screaming and shouting, and I had the lead and the collar, but no dog! And she disappeared for a few days; she'd gone somewhere, but she was found a couple of days later.

> (*Manchester at War: The People's Story*, p. 41)

Further out from the city centre, it was Hulme that received the worst of the Manchester raids. The compact terraced housing increased the likelihood of casualties, as bombs intended for Salford Docks, Trafford Park and the city centre targets went astray.

Maurice Cowan was drinking in the Beehive pub on Clopton Street when he heard the air-raid sirens. He decided to leave the pub and make for the underground communal shelters at the Alexandra Brewery, and as he was walking along Warde Street some three minutes later, the bombs began to fall. The Beehive was demolished, killing the licensee and the two people who had decided to stay to finish their pint. Fourteen people lost their lives in the nearby Manley Arms, where a wedding party was being held.

A view of the Shudehill/Miller Street junction after the raids. The ruins of Baxendale's

Another person who had a lucky escape from the same incident was Fred Davies. At the time a sailor home on leave, Fred was drinking in the Manley Arms when he heard the sirens. Whilst debating whether to stay for another pint, his wife appeared at the door reminding him of his domestic obligations. Fred relented and went with her – the best decision he was ever to make. He took shelter with his family in the basement of the Mulberry Street School, where he recalls hearing and feeling the explosions above him in the streets. When he emerged from the shelter he was shocked to see the wreckage, and the ARP men digging out bodies from the debris of the Manley Arms.

Sometimes a snap decision or a matter of yards or moments in one place or another was enough to determine life or death. Jean

are in the middle distance on the right. *(Greater Manchester Police Museum and Archives)*

Towndrow was just 7 years old at the time of the Sunday night Blitz. She lived in Dover Street, Hulme with her family, which included adored elder brother, 10-year-old Herbert. They were sheltering in the extensive cellars of the Cornbrook Brewery on the corner of Ellesmere Street and Trentham Street when the building took a direct hit which killed ten people. Her mother Emily was seriously injured and taken to the Manchester Royal Infirmary. Herbert was killed and Jean survived, simply because they had decided to swap places – bunk for bench – for the one night. Herbert was in the bunk area which was badly damaged. Jean relates: 'A woman who used to sit with us regularly had been thrown back against the wall. She was dead and her eyes were hanging out on her cheeks. There was stuff coming out of her mouth. It was terrible.' (*Manchester Evening News Supplement*, 5 September 1989.)

In the midst of the Hulme carnage there was the occasional piece of good news. About 100 yards away from the brewery, at the other end of Trentham Street under the railway line, Ken Harrop and three of his friends saw another heavy-calibre device fall. On seeing the parachute their first impulse was to run towards it to apprehend what they thought was a German paratrooper. Then they heard the clank, clank of the device's priming mechanism, and saw the 'great big thing … and it didn't look anything like a man'. (*North West Sound Archive.*) As they turned to run away, the bomb hit the railway embankment and detonated. Ken heard nothing, but the force of the explosion flung him and his friends down in the street. A few seconds later a thick cloud of earth and small stones from the embankment descended on them. None of the four was hurt, and it was clear that the slope of earth below the railway, by taking the brunt of the blast, had saved them.

Around a quarter mile to the south-east, early on in the raid an estimated 150 incendiaries had fallen, mostly harmlessly, on the open space at St George's Park (recently renamed Barracks Park). A stray one started a fire on the roof of nearby Midgeley's Soap Factory at 325 City Road. A factory worker recalled seeing a stream of boiling soap running down the middle of the road. The basement shelter of 200 capacity was evacuated and the fire extinguished with no loss of life. Further down City Road an H.E. hit Gibson's works off Erskine Street (roughly where the Shawgreen flats are now). Although 450 people were trapped in the overcrowded underground shelter, it was again evacuated and there were no casualties.

Further east, Chorlton-on-Medlock and All Saints had their share of damage and loss of life. The Manchester Royal Infirmary had already had its central stairwell demolished when it was the recipient of a parachute-borne oil bomb, drifting silently down out of the night sky. Auxiliary fireman Hugh Varah was later to tell about the hair-raising moment when the device 'came to rest against the chimney where it hung swaying on its lines, making a grating noise as it scraped to and fro against the brickwork'. (From *Forgotten Voices of the Blitz and the Battle for Britain*, pp. 393–4.) Then, at great risk to himself, Varah climbed up the debris to rescue two nurses, one of whom was in a coma and had to be carried.

The MRI and the adjacent nurses' hostel were the recipients of at least two heavy-calibre bombs, one of which was a delayed-action device which exploded just outside the building several hours later, creating severe damage. The nurses received praise for their calm continuation of duties, covering the patients to shield them from the dust and soot, and on one ward, dousing a live incendiary with sand. This last action prompted one of the grateful patients, John Price from Burnley, to write to the Lord Mayor recommending the Victoria Cross for the nurse involved. There was not a single casualty among the patients.

The nearby Eye Hospital was the scene of another heroic tale:

> Two patients in the Eye Hospital, as a result of the air raids, were the heroes of the rescue work …
>
> They are P.C. Prendergast and Aircraftsman Hexter, and were there when the bomb shattered three wards and the unused £10,000 Paying Patients' Home.
>
> Dr H. Grinyer and Nurse Holt were killed. Another doctor, Dr R.S. Scott, was trapped in the wreckage and the two men dug through a 24-inch wall and crawled along a tunnel, despite the fact that the building threatened to collapse on top of them. They eventually rescued Dr Scott after two-and-a-half hours – and then went on to help children, although they had not recovered from their own injuries.
>
> (*Spirit of Manchester*, p. 3)

Another hospital badly hit was the Jewish Hospital on Elizabeth Street in Cheetham Hill. Seven people, including five staff from the nurses' home, were killed when the shelter in the cellar suffered a direct hit from a heavy-calibre explosive. In the main building all the windows were smashed, and supply of electricity, water and gas was lost. Two maids trapped in the debris were rescued by a combined effort of nurses, staff, and even dancers from the nearby Cheetham Assembly Rooms still clad in their dance frocks and suits. The next day the patients, temporarily housed in the Freedman Hall, were ferried to Crumpsall Hospital.

Just south of the MRI an aerial mine destroyed most of Livingstone Street, which used to branch off High Street (now Hathersage Road, near Victoria Baths). Nine-year-old Annie Rowlands at No. 6 was buried alive in the debris with her mother for over three hours. Annie recalls that she had tried to work herself free of the rubble, but stopped when her mother said: 'Don't, you're hurting me.' Both mother and daughter were rescued and survived after hospitalisation, but Annie's grandmother had been killed in the initial blast. The explosion had killed four other people in the street, and many more in the close vicinity.

A few blocks north, on York Street, St Augustine's church was destroyed in the early morning by a parachute mine. There were three casualties, one of whom was the priest, Father George Street. One of the surviving clergy, Father Joseph Porter, helped by house-keeper Miss Toober, led twenty-five people to safety in the reinforced cellar. The surrounding area was devastated, rendering 341 people homeless. Across the city, over twenty churches were damaged, four of them put out of commission.

George Wood and his family lived in the nearby Grosvenor Square district in All Saints, and they usually took shelter under the build-ing known as the 'Scotch School' on the northern side of the Square, using the entrance on Lyceum Place. (This small road connected Lower Chatham Street with Lower Ormond Street, and the site is now partly covered by the vicarage of the new St Augustine's church.) On the evening of 22 December, however, there was no time to move to the deep shelter, so the family took refuge in the cellar of their home. After listening to the explosions up above for several hours, George's father decide to profit from what seemed to be a lull in the attack and go upstairs and – the sovereign Mancunian panacea – brew a pot of tea. Then the structure of the house seems to have collapsed, leaving George's father outside and the rest of the family trapped beneath the rubble and covered in brick dust in the pitch-black darkness of the cellar. They were taken out by the rescue services round about midnight. George remembers seeing Wilmott Street on fire, and the horrific sight of a fireman up a ladder, one moment silhouetted against the flames, the next obliterated by a fresh explosion. The family made their way to the next shelter, and another of George's vivid memories is the shrapnel pinging off the ARP warden's helmet and glowing on the pavement of Whittaker Street.

At 93 Higher Cambridge Street, Joseph and Sarah Ellis lived with their daughter Henrietta, familiarly known as Hetty. At the time of the raid Hetty's boyfriend, a soldier home on leave, was in the house. When the sirens sounded they all went down to the cellar, but, as often happened, at one point Joseph and Sarah came upstairs for something. That was when the H.E. fell. Unusually, the parents were trapped upstairs but survived, but Hetty and her boyfriend were killed outright, and buried so deeply that the bodies weren't found and identified until 30 December. For years afterwards, Sarah had the habit of touching her head, and picking up tiny and shining, but harmless, slivers of glass on her fingers.

Eastwards along Ashton Old Road, in Ardwick, a large aerial mine intended for the Ashton Road Goods and Mineral Yard struck the Royal Street/Prince Street district opposite the junction with Gorton Road. Jessica Martin remembers the damp cellar of her house which the family used as a shelter, the deafening noise and the shuddering of the room as the bomb fell, and the glass from the smashed windows rendered innocuous by the thick rubber blackout curtains. The next day she emerged to find Royal Street and Prince Street in ruins. Bodies, some of them so badly burned as to be unrecognisable, were being brought out by the rescue services. Harry Hardy, a young soldier on leave, searched through bricks and rubble with his bare hands, and eventually reached a mother and her small child, still alive.

Out along Hyde Road, in Gorton, three houses in Delamere Street were struck by an H.E. bomb. There were no casualties, but the explosion was so powerful it hurled a granite paving stone a couple of streets away through the roof of Wood's the bakers on the corner of Stanley Street and Abbey Hey Lane. Once again sturdy upholstery was the saviour, as the stone became embedded in an armchair in one of the upstairs rooms, whilst the family were unharmed on the ground floor. Peter Wood, nowadays landlord of a Denton pub, is a descendant of the wartime owners, and he recalls that the stone was kept for many years in the house's airing cupboard as a family memento of the Blitz. He says that 'ironically, it was about the size and shape of a 1lb loaf.'

Alan Lambert lived with his parents on Queen's Road near to Gorton Park, which was on the opposite side of Hyde Road from Belle Vue. One of the Luftwaffe targets was the world-famous Crossley Motors half a mile or so to the north, and Alan remembers seeing a batch of incendiaries burning in the park, and a red glow over the Crossley factory. He heard the pounding of the anti-aircraft guns on Melland playing fields, and remembers seeing shrapnel from the shells falling to ground. The Lambert family took refuge in the nearest communal shelter: a classroom in the nearby All Saints School which had been strengthened with sandbags. At around 9 p.m. the classroom was shaken by a massive explosion. It was the aerial mine which demolished Jessica Martin's Prince Street in Ardwick, a mile to the north-west.

Just to the north of the park on Gorton Lane the monastery, more correctly known as the Church of St Francis, was hit by several incendiaries, but they failed to find purchase on the steeply sloping roof, and burnt out harmlessly in the guttering.

On the far side of Great Ancoats Street, the community of Little Italy was having the worst of both worlds. Mussolini having backed the wrong horse by siding with Hitler on 10 June 1940, the Italian immigrant males had been deemed enemy aliens and carted off to an internment camp on the Isle of Man, leaving mostly women and children to suffer the Luftwaffe bombs. When the sirens sounded, the two underground air-raid shelters on Blossom Street became convivial, if fraught, meeting places. An incendiary fell on St Michael's church, but passed through the roof and burnt a hole in the floor without otherwise causing too much damage.

Elsewhere in Ancoats, on Rolleston Street, Barbara Nuttall was sheltering with her family under an upturned settee and chairs. A bomb fell close by, badly wounding someone two doors away, and Barbara remembers 'no windows in, and there was dust everywhere'. (*North West Sound Archive*.) The Nuttall family was unhurt, and transferred to the communal air-raid shelter, and from there to the Rest Centre at the Girls' Institute on Mill Street, close by Ancoats Hospital.

Further out along Rochdale Road, in Miles Platting, the cellar of the Foresters Arms on Pearson Street was used as a shelter. Beatrice

Potter, whose family ran hairdressing and drapery businesses on Pearson Street, spent the night of 22 December in the cellar. She emerged to see the street in ruins, and discovered that several of her neighbours were either dead or seriously injured. Her husband, a soldier home on leave, helped the rescue services to remove a little girl from the debris. The girl survived.

In the days when Rochdale Road and Collyhurst Road formed an acute-angled junction opposite Queen's Park, the Balmoral Hotel was the long, narrow building at the apex of the two roads. Teresa Lenari, whose Italian immigrant parents ran an ice-cream shop on Rochdale Road, spent the night of the air raids in the Balmoral, hearing the bombs fall and the salvoes from the anti-aircraft guns sited on the nearby patch of open land at Great Horrocks.

By midnight several extensive city-centre blocks were ablaze, and the sky above Manchester was glowing fiery red. Night had become lurid day, and the flames were so intense that people as far away as Stretford and Longsight claimed to be able to read a newspaper in the street, despite the blackout conditions. Five miles away in Sale, Town Clerk Bertram Finch recalled seeing 'what seemed to be the whole of Trafford Park and Manchester ablaze'. (*Trafford Archives.*) On the north side of the city, up the hill in Prestwich, Mary Corrigan saw 'every chimney stack, every church steeple … all silhouetted in the light of the flames'. (*North West Sound Archive.*)

Towards the end of the raid, around 5 a.m., there was a spate of high-explosive bombs, hitting Hulme, Chorlton-on-Medlock, and especially the area between Market Street, Corporation Street, and Shudehill. Another gas main was ruptured, with the inevitable consequences. Premises lost included Burton's Stores on Hopwood Avenue, Pifco Ltd, and Kenyon's Vaults, a pub later renamed the Old Wellington Inn. The telephone exchange on the top floor of the CWS Holyoake House on nearby Hanover Street was destroyed. This central incident was finally closed at 6 p.m. on Christmas Eve.

Also around 5 a.m. an incendiary fell on Victoria Station, injuring four people and putting some platforms out of use. The station, however, continued to function. Some more incendiaries set fire to the roof of Chetham's Hospital School, and the explosion which put an end to the nearby cathedral's Regimental chapel also broke the windows in the school. Worse was to come the following night. Fortunately the resident pupils had been evacuated to Cleveleys.

Another school hit that night was the new Manchester High School for Girls at Grangethorpe near Platt Fields. It had been open for just one term, and was almost completely destroyed by an H.E. After the Christmas holidays temporary accommodation for lessons was found in three houses in Didsbury, and for the rest of the war the remains of the Grangethorpe site was used as a storage space. Burnage Grammar School (as it was then) was hit by three bombs, wrecking the organ in the assembly hall, the gym, and the tennis courts.

The blitzed roof of the CWS building Holyoake House on Hanover Street. The in-house telephone exchange was destroyed. *(CWS)*

The remains of a car outside the partially destroyed Chetham's School on Christmas Eve morning, 1940. *(Manchester Evening News)*

The all-clear sounded at just after 6.30 a.m. on the 23rd, and dawn broke on scenes of widespread devastation. It was Monday morning, and despite everything people were still thinking of how they were going to get into work. The buses were running a partial service, turning back before they reached the city centre. Beyond this passengers walked between ruined or still burning buildings, accompanied by ARP wardens. They had yet to discover if their place of work was still standing.

Irene Pearson lived in Waterloo Road, Cheetham, and her route into work took her down Bury New Road and Great Ducie Street. She saw the broken windows of the shops, some of which still had fires in them, and a crater in the middle of the road. A parachute was strewn over the tram wires, suggesting that an aerial mine had caused the damage. She passed in front of the ruins of the Woolsack pub. The closer she got to the cathedral area, the worse was the devastation: piles of rubble and shattered glass covered the roadway, and everywhere there was the smell of burning. Eventually she gave up and went back home.

Frank Walsh recounts the following story in his autobiography *From Hulme to Eternity*. He made it into work at Abel Heywood's, a printers on Lever Street, between Piccadilly and Great Ancoats Street. One of his tasks on that morning was to deliver a package to an office behind John Rylands Library off Deansgate. He emerged into Piccadilly, and was confronted by the row of five-storey warehouses opposite him on Parker Street engulfed in fire. He was later to describe the spectacle as 'one mass of flames … like a backcloth to some giant inferno'. The fabric of the buildings on his side of the square was hot to the touch, and fire-men were hosing the brick and stone to cool it down. Frank changed his route to go down the wrecked Cannon Street, picking his way over debris and hoses. Fire tenders were still spraying water on smouldering shells of buildings. Each side street he came to was blocked, so his route to Deansgate was circuitous, across the river via Chapel Street, then down side streets, climbing over the rubble. When he eventually made it to his destination he found the printing firm in ruins and unoccupied. He returned to Abel Heywood the way he had come.

Librarian Izzy Wallman, after sleeping for a fitful hour or so beneath the cellar steps at home in Hightown, walked to the Central Library, worrying if he would be late for work. He relates:

> I had to walk the two miles to St Peter's Square as there were no trams running. Down Cheetham Hill Road there was shattered glass everywhere, windows blown out; on Miller Street the CWS building storing paint was blazing away; down the back streets fires were smouldering and there was the acrid smell of smoke everywhere. I got to the Library at ten past nine, ten minutes late, and the most astonishing thing was that there was a man sitting in the Reading Room reading a book as if nothing had happened.
>
> (*www.manchester.gov.uk*)

Bob Wild went into town from Prestwich with his brother, taking a meat and potato pie to his father who was involved with the rescue services. He recalls the smoking ruins of Deansgate with hosepipes snaking through the layer of water on the street, and parts of pianos blown out from Crane's music shop.

One worker tried to make his way down Miller Street beside Baxendale's store, but was stopped by a policeman. When asked why, the policeman pointed down the street. It was covered by a moving carpet of thousands of rats escaping from the still burning building.

Cannon Street after the Blitz. The Royal Exchange dome and tower may be seen on the right, and the Town Hall clock tower is central, in the distance. *(Kemsley Newspapers)*

Later that day the German High Command issued a communiqué which stated: 'During last night large formations of our heavy bombers attacked with great success the important industrial centre of Manchester. Large fires were caused in the factories and warehouses.'

This was of course an accurate assessment, but in the blasted city centre, work was continued if the office, shop, bank or commercial premises was still standing and useable, and sometimes even if not. William Arnold's on Upper Brook Street, manufacturer of aircraft parts during the war and motor car parts in peace time, had had its roof blown off. A temporary tarpaulin roof was hauled into place, and work carried on as before. Other businesses found temporary accommodation elsewhere, such as in the Ship Canal House on King Street. The partially destroyed Barclays Bank on Deansgate was simply relocated to their other branch on York Street. The Royal Exchange had been rendered unusable by a high-explosive device and fires from a shower of incendiaries, but a temporary Cotton Exchange office was set up on a street corner on Cross Street. It was reported that business was conducted with good humour, especially when the office workers were joined by a vendor of shoelaces. The Cotton Exchange was later re-accommodated in Houldsworth Hall (90 Deansgate, now Church House), one of the few buildings on Deansgate left relatively unscathed. A much-publicised photograph shows a cheery group of office workers bearing briefcases and bundles of files waiting on a pavement to be rehoused in other offices. The message was clear: Manchester was badly wounded, but still very much alive.

That Monday night the bombardment resumed, but the city was already better prepared. Fire brigade reinforcements had arrived: the manpower and equipment had returned from Merseyside, and fresh contingents had been drafted in from as far away as Oldham, Nottingham, Birmingham and Middlesbrough.

George Clark was a member of Eston Fire Brigade, near Middlesbrough. The call for five firemen and a trailer pump to go to Manchester came through at around 3.30 a.m. on the morning of the 23rd. By seven o'clock on the evening of the same day they were involved in the containment of the fires on Corporation Street. There was some initial difficulty because of the incompatibility of Teesside standpipes and Manchester hydrants, but this was solved when the newcomers channelled the water from a burst main. Despite the continuing hail of H.E.s and incendiaries, by early morning of the 24th the Corporation Street fire was under control. After quelling a blaze in a nearby block of shops, the crew were called to support the regulars at the major conflagration of the Portland Street/York Street/ Parker Street warehouses. It was now 5 a.m. George's section leader Stan Haggarth takes up the story:

A well-publicised photo of Manchester office workers showing the 'business as usual' attitude after the Sunday night's bombing. *(Manchester Evening News)*

I was suddenly pitched into a scene of six, ten, and twelve-storey buildings well alight. On one occasion … we had to take over from a crew who had all been killed, with the remnants of their gear still lying around. … We had to take over their equipment and carry on with the job they had been doing.

(Quoted in Hardy, *Manchester at War*, p. 84)

The all-clear siren had sounded at around 1.30 a.m., but fires continued to rage in several places in central Manchester, most stubbornly in the Portland Street district. What had appeared to be a fire under control suddenly flared up again when a strong north-easterly wind sprang up, carrying sparks and live embers from one site to another. To make matters worse, the pipeline from Godley Reservoir had been hit, greatly reducing the supply of water to the east side of the city. The problem was partially solved by running a long hosepipe from the Rochdale Canal on Aytoun Street to the blitzed areas. Obviously aiming for the extensive sweep of flames, the Luftwaffe had dropped further high explosives on the district. Another large blaze was started in the Silver Street/Chorlton Street area, and nine firefighters were killed by an explosion whilst attempting to quell the blazing Piccadilly buildings at the corner of Parker Street and George Street. There were also isolated reports of some Luftwaffe machine-gunners firing on fire brigade personnel: this is a story which occurs in so many narratives of various blitzes that one has to come to the unpleasant conclusion that it must have been true.

(*Manchester Evening News*)

The Teesside contingent worked non-stop for fifteen hours, a work rate which could be matched by both AFS and regulars of other brigades. They continued to battle the fires until Christmas Day, with minimal rest breaks and inadequate food. Co-operative Insurance Society worker Kathleen Knibb says that as she left her offices on Corporation Street on the Tuesday afternoon she saw 'exhausted firemen asleep on doorsteps and in odd corners' (from *An Epitaph for a Bygone Manchester*, p. 65). George Clark recalls a Christmas lunch of Oxo and two cream crackers. The Teesside squad were finally to return home to Eston early in the afternoon of the 27th.

The blaze in the warehouse district proved impossible to subdue without calling in the military. The Royal Engineers created firebreaks by dynamiting strategically situated buildings in Charlotte Street and George Street. (This involved demolishing the remains of the premises of the Literary and Philosophical Society.) At last, by the afternoon of Christmas Eve, the inferno had been shackled, and although still burning in isolated places, had stopped spreading.

Among the businesses damaged or destroyed in the Piccadilly area were:

Barlow & Jones	2 Portland Street	cotton fabrics
J. Templeton & Co. Ltd	2–4 Parker Street	carpets
Sparrow, Hardwick & Co. Ltd	107 Piccadilly	textiles
Peel Watson & Co. Ltd	6 Parker Street	textiles
Haslams Ltd	14–18 George Street	cotton fabrics
Brookfield Aitchison	22 York Street	drapers, hosiers, knitted goods
S. Finburgh & Son Ltd	101 Portland Street	calico printers
A. & J. Henry's	101 Market Street	department store

S. & J. Watts's wholesale store on Portland Street – now the Britannia Hotel – was saved from the worst of the incendiary fires partly by firemen using the heavy textiles material to smother the flames: a happy instance of the boot switching to the other foot.

Around midnight on the 23rd, Chetham's School was hit by an H.E., setting fire to the governors' private rooms and damaging the rooftops of the main hall and workshops. Fortunately the library of rare books was untouched. And help was at hand: on Christmas Eve, Lord Egerton of Tatton, one of the sponsors of the school, sent a squad of his estate workmen to help extinguish the fires and salvage over fifty pieces of valuable furniture. These were temporarily rehoused out of harm's way in Tatton Hall.

Another historic building destroyed by an incendiary was Cross Street chapel. The original building dated from 1694, when it was opened as a Dissenters' Nonconformist Meeting House. It was wrecked by a Jacobite mob in 1715, then rebuilt. An untended fire-bomb gutted the building on the second night of the Christmas Blitz. Amongst the celebrated artefacts lost was the triple-decker pulpit.

Outside of the city centre, once again it was Hulme that was the worst affected Manchester suburb. A number of high-explosive devices fell on mostly residential areas. Arundel Street near St George's church, just off Chester Road, was hit twice, with a few houses and Messrs Moorhouse Ltd works destroyed. Two people were killed.

The arches beneath Hulme Locks – the short branch canal linking the Bridgewater Canal with the Irwell, a few hundred yards from Arundel Street – had been made into air-raid shelters. Arch 32 received a direct hit from an H.E., killing two. During repair work most of the structure abruptly and lethally collapsed in domino fashion, workmen and horses being buried by around 2,000 tons of brickwork.

There was another direct hit on the Hulme Dispensary, which adjoined the Town Hall on Stretford Road, close to the Zion chapel and Rest Centre. Caretakers Mr and Mrs Capper and their daughter were trapped under hundreds of tons of rubble. ARP rescue workers spent fourteen hours tunnelling though the debris before reaching the Capper family. They then dealt with the extremely difficult tasking of bringing them out, crawling through the wreckage and shielding the family members against fresh falls of rubble.

Mary Jordan lived on Oswald Street, a block or two away from the Zion Rest Centre. Returning home from the shelter:

> We went round to Number 8 Oswald Street to find that the front of our house had been hit and was half down; there were no windows or chimneys. Worse was to come in Cooke Street. A gas main had gone and Mrs Bateman's house had blown up, killing her and three children. … Families had been wiped out, yet in the door frame of one house – all that was left of it – the fan light over the front door still had the glass intact with a crucifix still attached … It was a terrible time and the smell of fires which had been put out lingered for weeks. The air was murky and people were stunned …
>
> (*Hulme Memories*, p. 33)

The second night's attack was over sooner than the first – 171 air-craft as opposed to 270 – and the all-clear sounded five hours earlier. The probable reason for the Luftwaffe's departure was the returning cloud cover, rather than a display of Christmas spirit.

Over the two nights the official number of conflagrations – defined as major fires requiring lengthy and involved attention from a large number of personnel and resources – was six. A Luftwaffe pilot departing the scene in the early hours of the 24th reported count-ing five, but the discrepancy may be explained by the fact that by then the two separate blazes in warehouse blocks on either side of Portland Street would have coalesced into one.

An area of over 30 acres across the city centre had been turned into smoking rubble. In ruins were 165 warehouses, 150 offices, five banks and over 200 sundry shops and commercial premises.

On Christmas Eve Bessie Ross wrote to a relative in Australia: 'Manchester is now a martyred city. As I write these lines the centre of our town is still burning; hundreds of houses gone, and people

Firemen – mostly auxiliaries – try to contain the warehouse fires on Parker Street, Piccadilly. *(Manchester Evening News)*

homeless … We are thanking God night and day that we are still alive.'
(*Manchester Evening News*, 24 December 1940.)

The efforts of the firefighters and rescue services, whether regulars
or volunteers, deserve the highest praise. For example, one group of
AFS volunteers from Nell Lane, Withington, equipped with just one
10cwt pump, made their way across town putting out fires as they went,
ending up on Cheetham Hill Road some time after midnight. A study
of Appendix 1 will highlight the number of reiterations of 'Incident
closed' rubber-stamped soon after the initial report of the incident. Civil
Defence Records emphasise a similar repeated degree of success, with
the added indication of a readiness to continue the good work elsewhere:

Rescue party returned to depot from _____ Street. Fit for further
service.

Auxiliary fireman Arthur Stoakes was awarded the British Empire
Medal for gallantry. He was a motorcycle dispatch rider who rode his
bike for 104 hours through the worst of the Blitz, with petrol cans
strapped to his back. He was twice blown off the bike, and he stopped
six times to extinguish fires. Temporary Sergeant Andrew Whyte
also received the BEM 'for conspicuous gallantry; at a warehouse fire
[on Major Street, near Portland Street] when it became necessary to
evacuate, he climbed with a jet to the roof of the adjacent building'.
(*GMFS Roll of Honour*.)

Figures of Manchester casualties given by the Emergency Committee,
29 December 1940:

Fire Brigade	1 killed, 19 injured
Police	3 killed, 16 injured
Special Constables (War Reserve)	1 killed, 8 injured
Auxiliary Fire Service	11 killed, 72 injured
ARP wardens	4 killed, 26 injured

These figures do not include those killed or injured from the reinforcing
services (all AFS):

Nottingham	3 killed, 1 injured
Oldham	1 killed
Teesside	1 injured

The total number of Manchester civilians killed, including service personnel, in the two days of the Christmas Blitz was 376. Over 5,000 people had been made homeless, so the Rest Centres overflowed, with the result that eventually over sixty premises were used for temporary accommodation (see Appendix 4).

Despite all the destruction and disorder, the festive season was in most cases still celebrated, albeit in a reduced form. For example, the Co-operative Wholesale Society branch at Winsford in Cheshire supplied 4,000 meals consisting of hotpot servings, meat pies, sultana puddings and mince pies. They were prepared overnight on Christmas Eve and delivered to the Manchester Rest Centres the following morning, providing for those who had lost their homes at least a semblance of Christmas cheer.

FIVE

'LIGHTS AND FIRES EVERYWHERE': CHRISTMAS BLITZ (2): TRAFFORD PARK, SALFORD AND STRETFORD

- THE INDUSTRIAL ESTATE PREPARES: ATTACK AND DEFENCE •
- BLITZ AND RECOVERY •
- SALFORD AND STRETFORD BOMBED •

In 1940 Trafford Park was the biggest industrial estate in the world. Measuring 3 miles east to west, it had a working and residential population larger than present-day Carlisle. Upon the outbreak of war the estate was transformed into a hi-tech arsenal, and its massive productivity potential was not lost on the German High Command.

From May 1940 the Ford Motor Company was making Merlin XX engines for fighter planes Spitfires and Hurricanes, for de Havilland Mosquitos, and for Lancaster and Halifax bombers. Some 34,000 such engines would be produced by the end of hostilities. Hedley & Co. Ltd soap factory (later Procter and Gamble) supplied glycerine for the making of explosives, as well as the routine bars of soap – 10 million of them by the end of the war – for HM Forces. Parts for the Mulberry Harbour installations were provided by four different Trafford Park firms. Cable manufacturer W.T. Glover, who had first installed electricity in the Park at around the turn of the century, turned out Bailey Bridges, aircraft hangars, and a major section of the PLUTO fuel pipeline. Steelworks Taylor Bros switched their attention to gun bearings and parts for Churchill tanks. Thomas French on Chester Road made ladder webbing for ammunition pouches. British Alizarene, ICI, and Cowburn's supplied vital chemicals such as chloride for batteries, and the ICI plant was the first in the UK to produce penicillin in quantity. Dunlop added another factory to the one at All Saints and continued to construct barrage balloons. F. Hills & Sons manufactured 800 Percival Proctors, a monoplane used for training and communication purposes. The Co-operative Wholesale Society (CWS) constructed parts for gliders.

It would be an appropriate place to mention the immense part played by the British CWS in the war effort in general. We have seen their contribution to the supply of food, and it is worth noting that every rationing committee in the country included at least one CWS member. The cabinet works in Radcliffe started to make assault boats, and at Shieldhall in Glasgow the sheet-metal workers produced the 'flying dustbin', a bomb used in the D-Day landings. Battle dress and boots were supplied to the Armed Forces. (It may be significant, or at least of interest, that the totalitarian regimes in Germany, Austria, Czechoslovakia, Italy and Spain had banned the Co-operative Movement by mid-1939. For his fiftieth birthday Hitler had received a present from the Nazi party of 1 million deutschmarks – around £50,000 – filched from the liquidated Co-operative funds.)

In Trafford Park, Metropolitan-Vickers Electrical Co. Ltd were one of the most impressive multi-taskers, having a hand in the construction of:

Avro Lancaster Bombers (1,080 by the end of the war, in the new 800,000sq. ft factory west of Mosley Road)
Anti-aircraft guns and carriages
Magnetic mines
Radar equipment

Jet propulsion engines
Searchlights
Hand-grenade castings
Unexploded bomb defusing
Aircraft compasses
Gears for tanks
Contributions to initial work on atomic energy

The Metrovicks workforce was increased to a maximum of 30,000 during the war. Unsurprisingly for such a large and efficient organisation – tantamount to a whole community – defensive preparations were comprehensive and thorough. The firm had its own 1,100-strong fire service, 4,000-strong ARP unit, rescue squads and battalion of Local Defence Volunteers. A fleet of four ambulances was bought. The original outdoor air-raid shelters had been filled in following the false dawn of the 'peace in our time' episode, but then when war was declared better ones were dug, equipped and strengthened with railway sleepers. One of the tunnels was divided into storage space, assembly rooms, a kitchen stocked with iron rations, and a hospital with fifty beds and an operating theatre. Interior factory walls were reinforced at a cost of £7,500, a precaution which the Ford factory also invested in. The works gymnasium was transformed into a first-aid post with anti-gas cleansing facilities. Vitamin A and D tablets were made available to the workforce at a subsidised price. Thousands of steel helmets were given out free of charge. An in-house telephone system with central switchboard and forty handset points was installed, and there was a back-up system of communication using apprentices on bicycles should the telephones cease to function.

So intensive were the preparations that visitors from other companies and industrial estates came to inspect Metrovicks and borrow the ideas and infrastructure, in much the same way that Manchester's pioneering defensive measures had been taken on board by other civic authorities.

Ford, Hedley & Co. Ltd, Kilvert's and the CWS also had their own Local Defence Volunteers, and eventually the individual LDV sections were amalgamated into one Trafford Park battalion: the 'C' Company of the 45th County of Lancaster Home Guard. Hedley & Co. Ltd had their own underground air-raid shelters, shared with the Corn Products Company next door. Kilvert's constructed a

Metropolitan-Vickers Electrical Co. Ltd.
TRAFFORD PARK, MANCHESTER, 17.

State of "Emergency."

Should a state of emergency arise, the following procedure will obtain :—

AIR RAID WARNING.

The main Works buzzers will be used solely for the purpose of Air Raid Warnings, the signals being as follows :—

WARNING.—Intermittent short blasts of 3 seconds with intervals of 2 seconds for a total period of 2 minutes.

RAIDERS PASSED.—2 minutes continuous blast.

In addition to the Warning being given on the main buzzers, a similar Warning will be given on all the internal hooters, klaxons, etc.

DISPERSAL.

On receipt of the Warning, all employees must proceed in an orderly manner to their allotted shelters, and this movement will be controlled by the Wardens in charge of each group.

All employees must remain in their shelters until such time as the "Raiders Passed" signal is heard unless in the interval the presence of Gas has been signalled by the sounding of Rattles. In this case employees must remain in the shelters until they have heard the ringing of hand-bells indicating that the Gas danger has been cleared.

Every employee has been allotted a place in a shelter and in his own interest should be familiar with the number and location of the shelter and the route which has been arranged to reach same. In the case of any doubt on this point employees should get in touch with the Warden in their own Section.

At whatever hour a Warning is heard every employee must always go to the particular shelter to which he has been allotted with the exception of employees whose business takes them to various parts of the factory, and in this case such people will go with the group to which they are nearest at the time the Warning takes place.

In the case of men transferred from Nights to Days and vice versa, they must immediately on transfer get in touch with their Section Warden and make themselves familiar with the shelter to which they are allotted and the route to same.

The dispersal arrangements outlined above apply to all employees of the Company with the exception of A.R.P. personnel who will be on duty and who will report to their respective posts.

GAS MASKS.

Every employee must bring a Gas Mask to the Works and must have same available within easy reach on all occasions.

(Signed) **G. E. BAILEY.**
Director.

(Metrovicks)

sophisticated shelter three floors deep, with lighting system and radio and telephone links, and with a capacity of 250. Kilvert's also had a first aid and decontamination unit. There were nine shelters under the premises of the Carborundum Company abrasives and engineering firm, situated south of the lake and Trafford Park Road, almost dead centre of the estate. The Ford factory had a well-equipped subterranean first-aid post as part of its shelter system.

Trafford Park boasted its own internal railway system, at its greatest extent comprising 200 miles of track, with branch lines leading off to the freight loading bays of the biggest companies. Metrovicks took this idea one stage further by laying extra track from the workplace to the nearest air-raid shelter. This cost £340, and as it turned out, was money well spent. In some ways the estate was ahead of Manchester: water tanks had been constructed and ponds had been dug out and filled before the main attack, and temporary roads built to ease access to them. By mid-December 1940 the larger firms employed 'spotters' to watch for enemy planes. The 'spotters' system enabled employees to continue working even after the air-raid siren had sounded, leaving for the shelters only when the raiders were actually seen or heard. This meant that much more work could be done: it was calculated that the actual stoppage time was just 20 per cent of the 'red alert' periods, so that during the raids an estimated 600,000 man/woman-hours were gained this way. It is worth noting here that throughout the war no Metrovicks employee was killed on the factory site.

The Manchester Port Emergency Committee had been in existence since August 1939. Colonel T.H.G. 'Harry' Stevens, the Managing Director of Trafford Park Estates Ltd and son of the industrial estate founder Marshall Stevens, was the Warehousing member of the Committee, whose minuted intention was 'to keep the Port open and efficient'. One of their first tasks was to organise storage elsewhere for materials not essential for the war effort, so as to release space for more pressing needs.

Trafford Hall, which had been the stately home of the Trafford family for around 200 years before the coming of the Ship Canal and industry, was vacant apart from the caretaker and his family. Requisitioned by HM Forces – the caretaker was given just forty-eight hours to leave – it was now enclosed by a forbidding fence, given its first electricity supply, and used as a base for military training.

The estate was surrounded by a ring of anti-aircraft guns. These were positioned in Davyhulme Park, at Ackers Farm on Carrington Lane a mile or so to the south, in Westwood Park in Worsley, off Barton Dock Road in Lostock, and on a golf course in Kersal, Salford. Two machine-gunners were stationed on the Liverpool Warehousing roof near the north-east end of the Park, and one on the Kellogg's roof in the south-east, near where the Bridgewater Canal went under Park Road. There were two barrage balloons on the estate. Somebody hit on the idea of using the huge waste supply of oily rags to create a smoke screen. A line of concrete containers along Trafford Wharf Road was filled with wood shavings and paper, then topped off with a layer of the rags before being set alight. All these defensive measures, however, failed to stop the vast majority of German bombers wreaking havoc.

The target was too big, with too many salient features recognisable from the air, for it to avoid a severe mauling at the hands of the Luftwaffe. By October 1940 the famous Metrovicks water tower-cum-radio mast had been deliberately reduced to a 50ft stump – which served as another gun placement – but there were other tall landmarks, notably the two chimneys of Barton Power Station in the west, and the grain elevator by the Hovis factory on Trafford Wharf. And as in Manchester during the simultaneous Blitz, once the fires had taken hold, enemy aerial navigation at night was comparatively easy.

The 1 October attack on Trafford Park gave a taste of what was to come. The next major Luftwaffe raid began at around 6.30 p.m. on Sunday, 22 December, at about the same time that the first incendiaries were falling in central Manchester. Metrovicks worker Florence Myddelton was at home in Dane Road, Sale, looking northward from her bedroom window towards the estate: 'I just heard this sort of humming, like a lot of angry bees, and it came nearer and nearer and nearer, and then *thump! thump! thump!* and then you looked out and the flames were coming up …' (*North West Sound Archive*.)

At least sixteen H.E. bombs were dropped, along with hundreds of incendiaries. The eastern half of the Park was worse hit, with the largest factory – Metrovicks – taking a real battering.

Two 1,000lb parachute mines – dropped as usual in a pair – created widespread damage in the Metrovicks works, on both sides of Mosley Road. In the western works, a direct hit wrecked beyond repair the thirteen Avro Manchester bombers, just completed and ready for delivery. The staff canteen and heat treatment shop were also demolished. In the latter, worker and AFS member W.G. Dossett was buried by debris. Unaided, he made his slow and painful way to the first-aid station, where his wounds were dressed before he was sent home in an ambulance. He was back at his post by noon the next day.

Other Metrovicks departments destroyed were the gun mounting and switchgear testing works. Most of the principal machine shop was blitzed, and the main water supply was severed. The blast blew out the windows and roof glazing in the Meter Department and Pattern Workshop on the eastern side of the works. Below a tangle of twisted girders and wrecked machinery the floors were gouged out with huge craters, in remains of buildings that were open to the sky.

A few eyewitness impressions will serve to give the overall view of the degree of destruction across the estate.

Dennis Humphries recalled leaving the family Anderson shelter in Glastonbury Road, Stretford, and looking north to Trafford Park: 'It was like Blackpool illuminations, lights and fires everywhere' (*Manchester at War – The People's Story*, p. 30). From the Barton end, Kathleen Byrne was making her way with her family to the communal shelter in the basement of a mill on Patricroft's Trafford Road, when she looked across the Ship Canal towards the estate, and saw:

> … the blazing spectacle that was Trafford Park. Fires flared, and the red and orange of the flames lit up the night … It seemed as if half the world was ablaze. It must have been nearly half a mile away, but I could smell the acrid smoke and almost feel the heat and sparks from the inferno
>
> (*Workshop of the World*, p. 42)

John Clarke was an apprentice at Metrovicks, and one of his wartime tasks was to clear incendiaries from the flat roof. Using a 6ft-long scoop, he gathered up the burning bombs and dumped them into a large drum filled with sand. Once the device was quenched, it was then dumped over the side of the roof and on to the ground below. Unfortunately, on one occasion there was a huge number of bombs to deal with, and one member of the four teams on duty omitted to douse the incendiary properly before casting it below. The still live bomb landed on a pile of scrap magnesium, and 'the whole of Trafford Park lit up!' John recalls that later on the same night he could see an oil tanker ablaze on the Ship Canal away to the north, and that the whole scene was 'like Vesuvius erupting. It was unbelievable.'

James Atherton, in his part-autobiography *Home to Stay*, describes another view of the Park, from a Stretford street on the first night of the Blitz:

> At 6.40 p.m. sirens went followed by terrific gunfire …
>
> Fires burning over the dock area. Trafford Park factories on fire.
>
> All sky lit orange, red, pink. All quiet between guns. Dead silent.
>
> Always this stillness and silence …
>
> Just then more bombs landed on nearby industrial complex of Trafford Park. It sent along a cold breeze. Blast …
>
> Still not a soul in sight. Windows of houses reflect bright pink glow. Pavements pink.
>
> (Home to Stay, p. 27)

He goes on to say that later in the night the spectrum of colours was enhanced, depending on what was on fire in the warehouses and factories: chemicals gave off green and orange flames, whilst sugar-based fires were blue. He recalls that Cowburn's Chemicals near to the Bridgewater Canal was blazing fiercely, partly due to the highly inflammable carbon disulphide. The burning sulphur gave off a vile smell as it drifted southward on the breeze.

There were, of course, many other inflammable materials on the industrial estate: oils, gas, timber and grain were particularly combustible. The Hovis grain elevator was next door to Rosser's timber yard, which was on fire for weeks. The grain fire appeared to have been quelled, but for about six months after the Blitz it would flare up from time to time if the wind was in a certain direction.

Other firms suffering extensive damage were the American Oil Company which lost two oil containers and two warehouses; the Cold Storage Company lost its main storage warehouse as well as the three largest refrigeration units in the UK.

The Trafford Park Estates Annual Report gives the following properties as being completely destroyed:

A. B. & D. Warehouses, Trafford Wharf Road
Metropolitan Transport Supply Co.
Remer Timber Co. Ltd in Mosley Road
Rees Oils Ltd (Y.2 Warehouse)
Robert Wilson & Sons (X.2 Warehouse)

Three Ply Barrel Company (X.3 Warehouse)
U.F.P. (Hackney & Co.) Davidsons Building

The report then lists seventeen more premises that had suffered 'major and minor damage'. The addresses cover Trafford Park Road, Third Avenue, Mellors Road, Ashburton Road, Royce Road, and Westinghouse Road. Port of Manchester lost eleven of its twenty-four warehouses.

The Ford factory was strafed by twenty-five bombs, yet the number of casualties was kept low: according to the official figures, three killed and eight injured.

Trafford Hall was hit by an aerial mine, and the blast threw Tom Alexander, a soldier on duty, 30ft through the door of the ARP warden's office near the Lodge. Tom was treated for shock, but was otherwise unharmed.

In the nearby Hedley & Co. Ltd works a bomb fell through the factory roof and landed in a frame of soap two floors below. (A frame is a large container in which chemicals react to make soap.) The quick-thinking workers on the night shift pushed the frame into the lift and sent it down to the canal bank, thus saving the factory from heavy damage.

The next day being Monday, there was an influx of workers, despite the general ruin and the fact that many fires were still burning. Below Trafford Road swing bridge – where the eastern entrance to the Park was closed – some of the barges on the Ship Canal were in flames, and the metal of the bridge handrail was hot to the touch. Constance Howe, a Kellogg's worker, opted to try and get into work the long way round, via the southern entrance along Park Road. As she passed under the railway bridge near the junction with Barton Dock Road, she saw that: 'Anderson's across the road was burning fiercely. Metrovicks factory was blazing. The Kellogg plant was just standing there, among all that appalling death and destruction, practically untouched.' (*Workshop of the World*, p. 108.) The closest Kellogg's came was a UXB in front of the factory in Park Road, and an H.E. device which fell by the canal, creating little structural damage.

According to Co-op worker Bertha Armstrong, many of the CWS employees who arrived for work and saw the ruins of the factory on Trafford Wharf Road near the swing bridge broke down in tears. They were to be re-employed at the central Manchester CWS building on Balloon Street, which had suffered comparatively minor damage.

James Atherton of Stretford made a tour of the blitzed estate on his bicycle, accompanied by a friend. He saw craters in the roads, and many of the buildings in Trafford Park were still smouldering. A flour mill was still on fire, and the firemen who were playing hoses on the blaze were plastered with the dough which had combined with the water to make a sticky mess: 'Two firemen lay on the ground with burnt hands, their faces white with flour, eyes red-rimmed, like crumpled clowns.' (*Home to Stay*, p. 29.)

On his way back home Atherton passed Metrovicks, where his father had a clerical job. He noted that the office block where his father worked appeared unharmed.

Estate Manager Colonel Stevens also did the rounds on his bicycle, and later recorded the extent of the devastation. Three of the entries in his notebook were:

> Knowsley Cast Metal Ltd: All roof seriously affected, much glass and roof sheeting gone. In full production if weather fine, otherwise almost stopped.
>
> Brooke Bond & Co. Ltd: Considerable damage to roof covering and extensive glass damage. Building apparently badly shaken, details not available yet. All western doors displaced. Production normal.
>
> Northern Motor Utilities: Building only 50% sound, 50% of roof gone, remainder lifted and twisted. All glass damaged. In full operation.
>
> (Quoted Nicholls, *Trafford Park: The First Hundred Years*, p. 100)

One notes the positive tone of these observations: already thoughts are moving in the direction of what can be repaired and salvaged, and what still achieved. In the largest factories the shifting of debris and covering of damaged roofs and windows was begun immediately.

But there was more to come. The Monday night brought a massive incendiary raid, starting or reviving so many fires that even the large and well-equipped Trafford Park fire brigade was unable to deal with them all. Once more Metrovicks had the worst of it, this time a burning floor giving way with heavy machinery crashing through to the aisle below. The main machine shop was flooded with water and covered in rubble, making access difficult for firefighters.

Although the canals, lake and emergency tanks provided adequate water, there was a serious shortage of fire hose. This was eventually remedied by the arrival of three AFS units from Birmingham, and a lorry-load of hose from Wolverhampton.

Some incendiaries fell on the roof of a gasholder near to Barton Bridge. The danger was averted by the brave action of ARP Warden Henry Galgut, who climbed on to the gasholder roof and kicked the bombs off, one by one. There was another courageous act on the top of Barton Power Station, where Naval Lieutenant Dennis O'Hagan defused a parachute mine, with a fire raging close by. O'Hagan was later awarded the George Cross.

The central residential area was hit, with many houses damaged and seven on Eleventh Street completely wiped out. There were, however, no deaths or serious injuries amongst the residents.

The main underground telephone cable was severed, meaning that for two weeks communication was effected by apprentices on bicycles.

There are many individual memories of that time. Some of them perhaps reflected the fact that casualties were relatively few, and that generally morale remained high. The chief engineer of Corn Products was pleased to recall his minor brush with the Blitz. He was at his desk when a piece of shrapnel flew through the office window and landed, hot and glowing, smack in his in-tray. Alan Morrison, former worker at Metrovicks, tells the story of a Home Guard man walking through the Kilvert's abattoir during the blackout. He blundered into the carcase of a pig that had been hung up on a hook to dry, and ran out in a panic, shouting that there was a naked man in there who had hanged himself!

Another story emphasises the extent of the bombed area. Tom Marriott-Moore was in his office at Quick's Garages on Chester Road on the Tuesday morning when he spotted one of the apprentices walk past, with what looked like silk parachute cord in his pocket. The following conversation ensued:

'Where've you got that from?'
   'Oh, I've got it from the White City.' [This was a greyhound stadium on the opposite side of Chester Road.]
   'Whereabouts?'
   'Well there are some things hanging on the wire at the White City.'
   'Hanging by these cords?'
   'Yes, sir.'
   'Mm. Well you see that policeman by the Dog and Partridge? Go and tell him there are land mines in the White City greyhound track.'

(*North West Sound Archive*)

Luckily the apprentice had not cut down all the cords, or the outcome for the stadium and surrounding residential area does not bear
thinking about.

The Trafford Park Blitz had its heroes. Two firemen based at the
Stretford and Urmston station on Park Road were to be awarded the
MBE the following year. Chief Fire Officer Joseph Clitherow's cita-
tion 'for gallantry' contains the following:

> Showed devotion to duty and high qualities of leadership throughout
> enemy air attacks. Whenever conditions in the control room permitted
> he has visited the fireground and has directed operations in cases of spe-
> cial difficulty. By his determination and disregard of personal safety he has
> encouraged and inspired his men.
>
> (*GMFS Roll of Honour*)

Station Officer John Benn also received the MBE 'for meritorious
service':

> Displayed courage and coolness in dealing with a very serious situation
> when H.E. bombs had caused casualties among fire fighting personnel
> and members of the general public. He gave first-aid treatment and
> applied tourniquets to three badly wounded persons. He then went
> on foot, through intense bombardment, to the scene of other serious
> fires. He showed presence of mind and devotion to duty in extremely
> dangerous conditions.
>
> (*GMFS Roll of Honour*)

Tragically, John Benn's award had to be made posthumously in
April 1941, as he had been killed in the previous month's raid on the
industrial estate.

Patrol Officer David Whiteside received the King's Commendation
for dealing with fires and an unexploded bomb at the Ingersoll Rand
works during the 22 December raid. The same award was made to a
messenger from the Stretford and Urmston Fire Brigade for courageous duties performed during the air raid on Moss Park Road on
the 23rd.

After those two terrible nights, the Luftwaffe bombers did not
return en masse to Trafford Park, only in isolated incidents over the
next year or so (notably in the 9 January, 11 March and early morning

2 June 1941 raids) when the damage was less than in previous attacks. The German High Command then seems to have decided that the destruction was effectively total, and that the estate would no longer be making a significant contribution to the Allied war effort. How wrong they were.

One of the most inspiring stories of the Second World War is the rapid regeneration of Trafford Park Industrial Estate. Extra clear-up and decontamination squads were brought in from outside, and these were billeted and fed on site, in railway carriages loaned by the London Midland Railway Company.

Tools and equipment were obtained from far and wide, and within a week work was continuing, in many cases in premises minus a roof. Night shifts were obviously impossible because of the blackout restrictions, but in daytime open coke fires in braziers provided the warmth, as shop floor operations continued even when snow was falling. Alan Morrison recalls working in Metrovicks' machine shop wearing an overcoat and fingerless gloves. Francis Hogan relates that in the dynamo section, also at Metrovicks, he was back at work the day after the bombing, in a roofless building and on a floor ankle-deep in water from the fire hoses. He recalls:

> There was no way our spirit would have been broken, no way! We were always bloody singing, actually! I remember working where they were making harnesses for the Lancaster, and there was this guy and a female, and they used to sing a duet all bloody day long. ... We weren't really frightened, not to the extent of giving up the job, we were just normal people getting on with the job.
>
> (Quoted Phythian, *Manchester at War: The People's Story*, p. 53)

The Metrovicks West Factory, which had produced the short-lived Manchester bombers, was repaired and extended. The loss of the Manchesters ultimately proved to be something of a blessing in disguise, since production now switched to the superior Lancaster. Now equipped with four Merlin engines, the Lancaster was turned out at the rate of over forty-five a month, with a total of 1,080 reached by the end of the war.

Incredibly, within four weeks output in Trafford Park was back to 80 per cent of normal. It was estimated that by the end of the war 13 million tons of traffic had passed through the estate. To quote

Colonel Stevens's uplifting assessment: 'By good direction and hard endeavour, roads and railways were cleared of debris, and in quick time the wheels of the whole of the great Industrial Centre of Trafford Park were again turning and speedily attained a good momentum.' (From 'Summarised Annual Reports 1939–40'.)

Salford, like Hulme, suffered terribly in the Blitz, and for similar reasons: densely packed terraced housing and proximity to Trafford Park and the Docks.

One grim list will give an impression of the extent of the carnage. Among the whole families wiped out in Salford in the course of the Christmas Blitz alone were the following (numbers in brackets are the number of people in the family killed):

Ordsall

Aldcroft (4)	82 Oxford Street
Holmes (6 – including 9-month-old baby)	7 West Bank Street
Wilson (3)	20 West Bank Street
Wood (3)	11 Johnston Street
Davis (3)	11 Weedall Street
Moorhouse (5)	106 Bigland Street

Weaste

Barlow (4)	25 West Wynford Street
Brown (5)	Fumigation Station, Mode Wheel Road
Kennedy (4)	16 Darwen Street
Cassin (3)	31 Stowell Street
Cooper (3)	21 Milton Avenue

Pendleton

Ward (5)	28 Cook Street

Broughton Park

Cotterill (4)	55 Walnut Street
Midgley (3)	53 Walnut Street

Lower Broughton

Warren (3)	65 Nora Street
Bolt (2)	61 Nora Street

The grim job of clearing up: West Bank Street, Ordsall, Salford. *(Greater Manchester Fire Service Museum)*

The Bolts were a young couple in their twenties. The husband, William, was a Royal Artillery gunner home on leave. The Weaste casualties were nearly all from an area around the cemetery, a few hundred yards across the Ship Canal from Trafford Park, and less than a mile from No. 9 Dock.

The proximity of parts of Salford to central Manchester added to the likelihood of attack. The Exchange Station and the eastern end of Chapel Street, both in Salford, were separated from Victoria Station and the cathedral area by Victoria Bridge and a subterranean loop of the Irwell. To the north of Exchange Station, Greengate ended in one of the arches under the railway line. It was here that a driver of a double-decker bus decided to shelter during the 22 December Blitz. It was an understandable decision, yet it proved fatal. A high-explosive bomb passed right through the arch and demolished the bus, killing all five occupants: the bus crew and three passengers, one of whom was Doreen Gill, a 16-year-old girl from Bankfield Avenue, Longsight.

A mile to the south-west another Salford thoroughfare, Regent Road, crosses the Irwell boundary on its way towards the Knott Mill district of Manchester. Just below Regent Bridge, between the terraced houses on Wilburn Street and the river, was the Groves and Whitnall Brewery. As with the major firms in Trafford Park, Groves and Whitnall had constructed air-raid shelters and appointed wardens and firefighting squads. On Sunday, 22 December, however, the western half of the brewery was destroyed by a large bomb, the fires from which proved uncontainable for some days. Worker Allen Hayes relates what happened to him:

> This warden shouted to me, he said, 'There's something happening,' and somebody shouts, 'Look up! Look up!'… This warden must have known, so he shouts, 'Groves … it's a bloody landmine.'
>
> I took off down Wilburn Street … I got lifted off the floor, crashed down again, and I crouched there, and I could hear things falling over, and something fell, it must have been about as big as a house, and it crashed down not far away from me …
>
> Everything's battered, you know? Everything's dirty, smoke, soot …
>
> There were still guns going off and bombs falling, but they were more distant, you know. I walked on to Regent Road … I didn't know where I was, I stood there, 'Where am I? Where am I?' … That whole building had gone.
>
> *(Salford Life Times Oral History Collection)*

Casualties at Groves and Whitnall were the 70-year-old caretaker Mrs Mary Wilson Bentley, who had refused to leave her post at 1 Regent Road, and 33-year-old AFS fireman Robert Bunting from Higher Irlam. The blast razed most of the terraced housing in Wilburn Street, and a second bomb the following night hit the brewery again, reducing the office block to rubble. Regent Road was closed for three days whilst the debris was cleared, and the fire in the brewery smouldered for over a week. Nevertheless production continued even in the roofless and cold conditions.

Further up Regent Road, Norma Sincup's family ran a butcher's shop. When the air raid began it was the father's idea to switch off the power to the shop's walk-in refrigeration unit and for the family of four to shelter in there. It proved to be a good choice of action, as when they emerged at the all-clear cold but unharmed, the whole shop had been destroyed, with only the fridge left standing.

Beyond the crossroads of Regent Road and Cross Lane (where the roundabout at the end of the M602 is now) was situated the terraced

The Groves and Whitnall Brewery after the Christmas Blitz. In spite of the
devastation, on-site production continued. *(Greater Manchester Fire Service Museum)*

housing of the Woodbine Street area. During the first night's attack,
residents were moved to shelters along Liverpool Street, past the gas-
holders which were on fire through incendiary bombs. On top of one
60ft-high gasholder, a jet of flaming gas was issuing from the punc-
tured crown, threatening to spread the fire on to adjoining buildings.
Fireman Charles Bigland of the Salford Brigade climbed on to the
roof of the gasholder and, lying full-length, managed to direct the
hose water into the gap, thus extinguishing the fire. He was later
awarded the BEM for his brave action.

South of Regent Road, sandwiched between the Salford and
Pomona Docks, lay the densely packed terraced houses of Ordsall.
Of no military importance – unless you counted the cotton mills and
timber yard on Ordsall Lane, and the iron and engineering works
on the riverbank – nevertheless, due to its unfortunate position, the
district drew a lethal wave of bombing. Irene Pope, who lived on
Trafford Street, backing on to St Bartholomew's School, which was
on the corner of Derby Street and Tatton Street, recalls witnessing at
close quarters the fall of a parachute mine:

> Suddenly this mine came floating over the school yard. It was losing height but we realised it was heading for the houses next to ours which had attics, so they were a storey higher than ours. Suddenly a gust of wind came. It seemed to twist the parachute and took the mine over our house, missing the next one literally by inches.
>
> (*MEN Correspondence*, 28 February 1998)

However, the tragic outcome was that the mine landed on the ARP post on Ordsall Lane, killing all the occupants.

Betty Morris (née Toy) lived on Bigland Street, off Ordsall Lane. When the bombs started to fall she hid with a friend in the coal place under the stairs, but when the house shook with the detonations they decided to make a run for it to the air-raid shelters in the stables on Oldfield Road. She remembers neighbours shouting to her to get back inside, but she ignored them – a most fortunate choice of action, as it turned out, as Betty and her friend arrived safely at the stables, but Bigland Street was later flattened by an aerial mine, with great loss of life.

Henry Abraham lived on West Union Street, and worked at the cotton mills on Ordsall Lane. One of the places where he worked, Egerton Mill, was completely gutted, and Henry recalls: 'All along the Irwell the barges were cut from their moorings and were on fire. The warehouses along the canal were lit up and well ablaze, as well as the streets. It was really terrifying, and anyone who said he was not frightened was lying.' (*Memories of the Salford Blitz*, p. 16.)

In the midst of the mayhem, one of the oldest buildings in Greater Manchester remained mostly untouched. The fourteenth-century Ordsall Hall, a couple of hundred yards away from the burning mills, the canal and the Pomona Docks, survived the bombing, along with its grounds which had been turned into allotments for growing food.

West of Cross Lane and north of Eccles New Road is the district of Pendleton. Here is where Albert Armstrong lived, on Buckingham Street, near to the junction with Hodge Lane where there was Bocock's the corner shop. Situated in the midst of inflammable materials – the Bradford Dyers' Association works took up one side of the street, and mattress and firelighter factories were close by – the area was highly vulnerable once the incendiaries started to fall. Albert remembers the scream of the bombs, and 'massive explosions everywhere'. The residents were moved by an ARP warden and a policeman to an air-raid shelter in St Ambrose's School on Liverpool Street a couple of hundred yards away. Here Albert recalls someone calling out: 'They've hit the church!' whereupon he climbed on to a bench to look out of the school window: 'I remember seeing just a thin wisp of smoke coming out of the slates on the roof [of St Ambrose's church]. Then suddenly, with an almighty whoosh, all the windows of the church exploded outwards and the lovely church where I was christened was engulfed in flames and completely gutted.' (*Salford Life Times Oral History Collection*.)

Mary Dutton was witness to an aerial mine falling on the Pendleton terraced street of Highfield Road, and the houses 'toppling … like a deck of cards'. Surrounding streets were damaged too, and she recalls seeing people with 'faces black with soot' and 'covered in slutch and other debris'. (*Memories of the Salford Blitz*, p. 13.) A row of shops, a bank, a Chinese laundry and a pub were destroyed on Church Street and the section of Broad Street near to St Thomas's church.

To the north of Pendleton there is the former semi-rural village of Irlams o' th' Height. Mostly invisible now beneath the roundabout and dual carriageway, in 1940 vestiges of the village remained with St John's church (still there alongside the pell-mell of the present-day traffic), the local school, and the half-timbered Pack Horse Hotel. Although there were no casualties, and Blitz damage to property was minor compared to other parts of Salford, the incidents are worth recording. Elizabeth Watson (née Rouse) relates that she was with five other people in the family's well-appointed surface shelter when a bomb fell: 'We were comfortable there with an electric fire, electric kettle and supper trolley until there was a terrific whoosh! – the blast from a nearby landmine, which sucked the inside out of the house.' (*Salford life Times Oral History Collection*.)

At the all-clear Elizabeth entered the house to see that the roof had gone, and to find that the electricity had been cut off. In true British tradition, she went looking for a cup of tea. She found one in the mostly undamaged Pack Horse, where the landlord Mr McLusky was happy to supply the service.

Close by, the church had lost its roof and doors, and the stained-glass windows had been blown in. Houses in the Bank Lane area had also had their windows smashed, but it is thought that this was the result of the blast from the anti-aircraft guns stationed across the railway line in the Park Lane Farm fields. After this attack – once again being wise after the event – village fire-watchers were organised into two teams: one for the church, and one for the school.

The village had its part to play in the post-war rehousing: by March 1946, 216 permanent concrete homes would be constructed along Duchy Road.

Less than a mile south of Irlams o' th' Height, just outside the front door of No. 7 Seedley Park Road, a UXB buried itself 20ft down into the pavement. It was a timed device, set to go off several hours later. Mrs L. McGuire, who lived with her family at No. 7, recalls that the ARP wardens cleared the street immediately, and the residents ran to the nearby Buile Hill Park, where there were underground shelters. The bomb exploded the following night, and the McGuire family, having lived temporarily in Langworthy Road School cellar, were later billeted in a house in Alpha Street West, just round the corner from their original home.

The impact of another such delayed detonation device was witnessed on Eccles New Road by Mr E.N. Walker, a member of the Cross Lane Home Guard:

> On the main road one [bomb] went through the roof of Bargains Unlimited, which occupied two shops. When we went inside we could see the fins of the bomb in the cellar. We told the Air Raid Warden about it, but he wouldn't believe us because when he looked the bomb could not be seen. It was a new type which had a vibrator in it and the bomb had gone down into the rubble. At seven o'clock the next morning there was a dull bang and the building just folded up like a pack of cards.
>
> (*Memories of the Salford Blitz*, p. 19)

Down along Eccles New Road, beside Stott Lane, Hope Hospital was hit by a parachute aerial mine. Among the casualties were Dr John Giles, his wife Annie, the Matron Mary Jane Ross, and Fire-watcher Norman Hertzog. No patients were lost, however, and the hospital was able to resume normal functioning within a couple of days. The memorial stained-glass window dedicated to Mary Ross is now in the chaplaincy at the new Salford Royal Hospital, which is on the site of the former Hope Hospital.

South of Seedley, between Eccles New Road and the Docks, is the district of Weaste. As with Ordsall, its unfortunate position drew the bombs. One survivor was a Mr R. Gorton, who relates that a 500lb

UXB caused the whole of Smyrna Street to be evacuated to the shelter at Weaste Congregational church, where the residents remained until Boxing Day. The worst bombing was on Mode Wheel Road, where the Fumigation Station suffered a direct hit, with several casualties. Gravestones in Weaste Cemetery still bear the marks of Blitz damage.

North of Chapel Street and the lower Irwell loop, the district of Lower Broughton received a significant share of the bombs. On the left bank opposite Peel Park and the David Lewis Recreation Ground, where industrial targets appear to have been the Dyeing and Finishing factory and the Copper Works further downstream, the terraced housing was badly hit, with many casualties. Areas around Bridge Street and Nora Street, and further north, around Irwell Street, were worst damaged.

The raw figures will give an overview of the dreadful reality of those two nights in Salford:

Number of H.E. bombs		276
Number of incendiaries	(appx.)	10,000
Number of major conflagrations		1
Number of major and smaller fires		431
Civilian fatalities		197
Civilians seriously injured		177
Fire, police and rescue services:		
	Fatalities	18
	Injured	85
Houses destroyed or damaged	(appx.)	8,000
People rendered homeless	(appx.)	20,000
Schools suffering major or minor damage		67

(Details taken from *Our Blitz*, pp 22-26)

On the plus side, by summer 1941 some 18,000 of the homeless had been billeted elsewhere, 1,200 were staying temporarily with friends or relatives, and new homes had been built for 2,225 people. Once again, in the long term the infrastructure was to prove stronger than Hitler's bombs.

A major military target in Salford was, of course, the Docks. On the morning of the 23rd Jake Abram, 15 years old at the time, left the disused Manchester and Salford Junction Canal tunnel shelter below Grape Street (near to Prince's Bridge, on the Manchester side of the Irwell) and boarded the tug *Preston* with his father: 'As we went down the Irwell, Lloyds warehouse on Water Street was burning. It was a big warehouse, full of foodstuffs and all sorts; the lard had melted and it was still on fire, running down the wall and on to the water.' (*Tugs, Barges and Me*, pp. 13-14.)

The tug passed by the opened swing bridge on Trafford Road, and tied up in No. 7 Dock next to the fire tug, MSC *Firefly*. On the Ship Canal burning barges were drifting free from their moorings, and across the canal to the south, Trafford Park was a smoking wreck. Jake Abram relates that he scrambled over a tarpaulin sheet on the *Firefly* without giving it a second thought, until a soldier on duty informed him that there was an unexploded bomb beneath it! The device was defused by the bomb disposal squad later that day.

Among the merchant ships sunk in the attacks on the Salford Docks was SS *Stella* with its cargo of pig iron, hit during the following 11 March raid. The official handwritten record of incidents notes that three ships (unspecified) were sunk in this attack. That was a bad night for shipping at the Docks: besides the three craft lost, five more cargo boats or liners suffered damage. The SS *London II* had its antimine equipment destroyed through incendiaries. Two gunners on the merchant ship *Hardwicke Grange* were killed by machine-gun fire.

It was also this 11 March raid which caused severe damage to Ladywell Sanatorium, Hope Hospital again, and Eccles New Road flats. Margaret Robinson (née Morris) was 6 years old at the time, a patient with scarlet fever in Ladywell Sanatorium:

> When the sirens went the nurses rushed round and pulled the mattresses, bedding and patients off the beds and pushed the whole lot under the beds and there we lay – terrified! Parts of the hospital were bombed and the blast brought down the paper black-out blinds. We were convinced we were being invaded by German paratroopers.
>
> (*Memories of the Salford Blitz*, p. 18)

The Docks were hit once more on the night of 7–8 May, with No. 7 Dock and the wharf railways badly damaged. Although no ships were destroyed in this attack – four large merchant ships had narrow escapes from UXBs – the oil installations on both sides of the docks were set ablaze. Some tanks of whale oil were ruptured, and some of the burning oil flooded on to the canal banks before being contained.

Ruins of Hope Hospital, Salford, after the March 1941 raid. *(Kemsley Newspapers)*

Salford suffered cruelly again on the night of 1–2 June, the last severe raid experienced by the city. The Royal Hospital on Chapel Street received a direct hit, and amongst the casualties were fourteen probationer nurses. Two nurses who survived were trapped in the debris before being rescued by Salford Fireman Edwin Irwin and AFS member Fred H. Smith, who had to crawl beneath the wreckage to reach them. One of the nurses had to have her arm amputated so as to free her from under the debris. Irwin received the British Empire Medal, and Smith was awarded the King's Commendation.

Close by the hospital, the area around St Philip's church was bombed once more, and a colleague of Canon Peter Green, 44-year-old Reverend John Hussey, was killed as he was making his way from the church to his ARP duties.

Altogether forty-four Salford people lost their lives during this attack. Among the premises damaged were Threlfall's Brewery, Bloom Street Gasworks off Chapel Street, Wheeldon's Timber Yard on Regent Road, and the Exchange Station. At the gasworks an H.E. bomb and a hail of incendiaries caused raging, contending fires.

Hero of the incident was Deputy Manager J.E. Wakeford, who after rendering the gas supply safe and containing the flames with some impervious clay, stayed at his post until a firepump was made available. Later that year he received the OBE for his courage.

The record of bombing incidents in Salford gives a total of 261 fatalities during eleven major raids on the city. The last Salfordian to die from injuries sustained during the Blitz was James Henry Redgrave, an octogenarian fire-watcher of Howard Street, who was severely injured whilst performing his duties at Kenyon's on Victoria Bridge on 2 June 1941. He died aged 86 in Salford Royal Hospital in January 1947. War casts a long shadow.

Stretford suffered the same fate as Salford and Hulme. Its proximity to Trafford Park, the Pomona Docks and two major railway arteries meant that stray bombs aplenty strafed the residential areas along with the original military and economic targets.

The most crucial strike was in the early hours of 23 December, when a high-explosive bomb demolished the police station on East Union Street. Not only were six policemen killed, but the hit was a devastating blow to the town's communications and defensive infrastructure. At a stroke, vital telephone links with the ambulance depot

Ruins of the original Salford Royal Hospital on Chapel Street. *(Greater Manchester Fire Service Museum)*

on Empress Street, the rescue party depot on Wright Street, and the Manchester Town Hall, were destroyed. Until alternative police premises were set up in a nearby street, heavy demands were made on car, bicycle and foot messengers.

Churches and schools were badly damaged. Worst hit of the churches was All Saints' on the corner of Cyprus Street and School Road. Damage amounting to £20,000 was recorded, and one report told of 'a mass of charred timbers'. Whilst the roof was still ablaze, firemen managed to save the cross, candlesticks, and some small pieces of furniture. The church was rebuilt after the war and relocated on Barton Road, by the railway bridge. St Peter's at Gorse Hill had its altar and east end completely blown away. Also in Gorse Hill, the Stretford Girls' High School lost one whole wing.

On the second night of the December Blitz, a couple of hundred yards south of the Trafford Park factories, nearly every house in Melville Road was flattened. Round the corner in Lyndhurst Road, two gruesome details will suffice to give an impression of the horrors suffered by the civilian population. A lady lost her arm in the initial H.E. blast, and firemen had to amputate a young lad's foot with an axe in order to rescue him from a collapsed building. Both victims survived.

Also on the Blitz's second night two of the most serious incidents occurred. The first one reflects the intensity of the high-explosive bombing, as no less than six H.E. devices were dropped on or around the Victoria Park residential area. One of them demolished part of Victoria Road, three exploded in the park itself, and at least one scored a direct hit on the surface shelters by the school, killing all occupants. A couple of miles to the north-east, by the Trafford Public Baths, Stanley Road (formerly Cooke Street) was hit by an aerial mine, causing thirty-three deaths.

Official records give an indication of both the hardships and the heroism in evidence in Stretford on those two horrendous nights. Appendix 2 shows the concentration of the raids, with a hail of incendiaries closely followed by dozens of high-explosive devices across the district. A total of 229 separate incidents were reported. And we should note the subsequent awards, a high number for such a small area: two George Medals, ten British Empire Medals, three MBEs and five King's Commendations.

There is a memorial to the town's civilian dead in Stretford Cemetery. The inscription reads: *This Garden is dedicated to the memory of the residents of Stretford also seventeen unidentified persons who lost their lives through enemy action in December 1940 and were interred here. May they rest in peace.* (See Appendix 2.)

The following Stretford buildings were also hit by Luftwaffe bombs during the December raid:

Henshaw's Institution for the Blind
County Police Headquarters, Old Trafford
Globe Cinema, Old Trafford
Lancashire County Cricket Ground
Welsh Church, Old Trafford
Unitarian Church, Old Trafford
Old Trafford Public Baths, Northumberland Road
St Joseph's R.C. School
Lostock School
Park Road Post Office
Corona Cinema
Metrovicks Social Club, Moss Road

(*Our Blitz*, p. 27)

Besides the casualties and damage to buildings, most of the residents had to suffer a lack of electricity and running water for two weeks.

The raids on Stretford did not end with the New Year. The following 11 March saw the town attacked once again. During the three hours' bombing the major target seems to have been the area around Pomona Docks, Cornbrook railway sidings, and Trafford Wharf. A ruptured gas main on King's Road created a blaze which guided later waves of bombers.

This was the attack which wrecked Manchester United's ground at Old Trafford. Harry Frost, a member of the ARP squad based at Trafford Road Mission, Salford, was actually positioned under one of the pitch crossbars during the raid, and he recalls a shower of incendiaries falling on the grass and setting it on fire. The main centre stand, the dressing rooms and medical room were destroyed. There was a total of around £50,000 damage. It would be August 1949 before the stadium could be used again for League and Cup football. In the meantime, United's home matches were played at City's ground at Maine Road.

Given a safe distance in time, jokes borne of tragedy may, on occasions, legitimately surface. The one going the rounds in the 1990s was that it was the grandfather of the German Manchester City player Uwe Rösler who had flown the Heinkel which dropped the bomb on Old Trafford. Not true, of course, but a good joke nonetheless, and as they say, laughter is sometimes ultimately a great healer.

SIX

'MANCHESTER TOOK IT, TOO': AFTERMATH

- PICKING UP THE PIECES, JANUARY 1941 •
- INQUEST ON THE RAIDS •
- FIRE-WATCHERS • REST CENTRES •
- BLITZ BARGAINS AND COMPENSATION •
- THE US VIRTUAL PRESENCE •
- LATER LUFTWAFFE ATTACKS •
- MORALE AND A MOCK INVASION •
- THE MISCONSTRUED LEAFLET DROP •

The chapter's title is taken from the 1941 CWS film of the Manchester Blitz, a ten-minute documentary whose title is itself a nod towards the *London Can Take It* movie, which was coincidentally released in the same week as the Christmas raids on Manchester. The CWS film is these days catalogued as 'propaganda', which suggests a shadow of doubt as to its accuracy. This seems an unfair label, as the images and narrative of destruction, determination to carry on with work, and beginnings of renovation are authentic. What grates on modern ears is some of the racially reductionist soundtrack: 'Here one may study something of the genius of Germany' from the voice-over as the camera pans across a smoking ruin does not sit well with peacetime politically correct views. The ending is upbeat: to stirring music and a shot of buses running, we are told: 'A new city will arise.'

Manchester Took It, Too may be viewed at the Central Library 'Archives Plus' section, and on the CWS website.

A new city did indeed arise from the rubble, but it would take many years to complete the job. Although the very worst was over with the end of the Christmas Blitz, sporadic raids of varying degrees of intensity continued for over a year. The immediate scenario remained grim.

A mass funeral for the Manchester Christmas Blitz victims was held at the Southern Cemetery on Saturday, 28 December. The Bishop of Manchester conducted the service, and representatives from the police, the fire brigade, the hospitals and the Civil Defence were in attendance as a bugle sounded The Last Post through the morning air.

The New Year brought no relief. On the evening of 1 January, Gorton and Withington were bombed, with several casualties. An Anderson shelter in the back garden of No. 15 Tealby Road, West Gorton, suffered a direct hit from an H.E. bomb which wiped out the whole family. Norman Williamson recalls watching Fred Astaire in *Broadway Melody of 1940* at the Scala cinema in Withington when the air-raid warning came on the screen. As often, nobody left their seat during the performance. However, after the film had finished Norman was walking home with his friends on Burton Road when an ARP warden told them to get in the shelter near The Old House pub. They refused, preferring to risk the walk home. The next day they discovered that the shelter had received a direct hit from a parachute mine, killing everyone inside. Victims included two ARP wardens and a local dentist.

Not all the news from the home front was bad: St Paul's church, also in Withington, received a parachute mine, but the device became entangled in a churchyard tree without exploding. According to Eileen Towers, Withington resident at the time, local tradition had it that the deceased former vicar of St Paul's, the doughty old Reverend William Muzzell who had been rector for forty-seven years until his death in 1939, was exerting his celestial influence!

One week later, on Wednesday, 8 January, there was held a public meeting at the Town Hall to assess the state of affairs. The next day the *Manchester Guardian* gave a fair summing-up: '... although there was criticism on details, there was nothing but praise for the personnel in all the departments which served the city devotedly during and immediately after the vicious attack.'

For example, there were 'the men of the firefighting services who, though dead tired, worked for hours under bombing attacks'. It was noted that over 72,000 meals had been served in the Rest Centres during the week of the Christmas raids. Praise was expressed for those who had maintained public transport. Mention was made of six civilians and one soldier who had dealt with over forty incendiary bombs and stopped many fires. Sir R. Noton Barclay spoke of 'an epic of fine heroism worthy to rank high … in the annals of the city of Manchester'. Despite the generally positive reports, there were expressed three areas of concern: on-site early warning of fires, whether the Rest Centres could cope with another influx of homeless, and the plans for rehousing of the bombed out.

To a large extent due to the experience of Manchester, fire-watching was soon to become a national legal statute. All civilian males between the ages of 16 and 60 were obliged to register for fire-watching duties of a total of forty-eight hours per month. By April, 20,000 men were registered in Manchester. Once the law was in place, punishment for neglect of duty – or worse, being drunk at one's post – was severe, involving a heavy fine or even a prison sentence. Every large building, office and shop in the city, whether occupied or not, had to have a full rota of fire-watchers. Originally this was for twenty-four hours a day, but daytime duties were being phased out by the summer of 1941. To help those whose shift straddled Saturday night and early Sunday morning, a special bus and tram service was run from Albert Square and Piccadilly from 7.30 a.m. on the Sunday. Later on in the year the Emergency Committee organised sleeping and catering facilities for those on fire-watch in empty office buildings. Pay was a token 1s 6d for up to five hours, and 3s for anything over that.

The Emergency Committee suggested the following measures for the 3,000 city-centre businesses deemed at risk: fire pickets patrolling the streets, a 100-gallon water tank on each floor, and windows protected with asbestos (obviously this was before the health hazards associated with the material were generally known). The Chamber of Commerce acted as liaison between the fire brigade and the major firms. It is not recorded how many of the 3,000 actually complied with all recommendations, but now, having had the bitter experience of the Christmas Blitz, Manchester commerce was certainly better prepared for the next attack.

Each district organised itself into a 'good neighbours' fire-watch scheme. Withington, for example, were proud to publicise the fact that over 100 shops, business premises and civic buildings, from the library to the White Lion pub, had designated fire-watchers. Local window-cleaners, builders and decorators had loaned ladders and handcarts, and stirrup pumps had been purchased (at £1 a time) from the Town Hall. Burnage reported that their Defence Force had 400 stirrup pumps for 1,000 homes, and they had applied for more equipment. The local voluntary scheme, amid some controversy, was about to be dissolved and reorganised into the aforementioned nationally run system, with each individual and his responsibility named and registered, but the effectiveness was not diminished, if the official records are to be believed.

Responding to the reports of the occasional difficulty in accessing water, the Manchester Fire Brigade compiled a census of all water sources in the city: ponds, lakes, streams, swimming baths, canals and rivers were located and catalogued. These would soon include the open tanks by Piccadilly, where the basements of the demolished

Open water tanks in Piccadilly, replacing the demolished Parker Street warehouses. Also visible are the communal surface air-raid shelters. *(Greater Manchester Police Museum and Archives)*

Parker Street warehouses would be filled with thousands of gallons of water. Pieces of advice were circulated, usually via a local newspaper: test your stirrup pump every morning, and if you use a ladder in your job, don't lock it away at night, but leave it out in the street, where it can be found and used if needed for firefighting purposes.

The meeting then turned its attention to the Rest Centres. It was accepted that part of the problem of overcrowding was down to people entering them who should have gone to a shelter, and a partial solution was to increase the number, and improve the condition, of public shelters. As one councillor put it: 'Provide more shelters of a better type, and there will not be this stampede for Rest Centres.' The transformation of communal shelters will be covered in the next chapter.

As for the Rest Centres themselves, more were to be created and appointed. Eventually there would be a total of sixty-five, including the overflow premises that had been used just once or twice (see Appendix 4). Here the bombed out would receive food and a hot drink, a place to sleep – by January 1941 bunks, blankets and mattresses had replaced the deckchairs – and even, in extreme cases, clothes, shoes, and money. (As we will see in the next chapter, those who misappropriated these and similar facilities received heavy punishment, usually involving a prison sentence.) Each Centre was to have an experienced person in charge, 'used to dealing with groups of working-class people'.

The next item on the meeting's agenda was the question of repairs and rehousing. One of the first tangible results of this was the provision to the needy, by Autumn 1941, of crockery, cutlery, blankets and cooking utensils from Manchester Corporation, plus (from the government's central stock) a supply of 'plain deal furniture' which included beds, wardrobes, two-tier bunks, chests of drawers, food cupboards, and chairs. Windows would be available from the stock originally intended for the projected houses on the Wythenshawe estate.

By early summer the Emergency Committee had requisitioned 250 privately owned vacant dwellings, which would accommodate over 1,000 people. The premises included twelve ten-roomed houses 'in the £750 class' in Whitworth Park, property of a schoolmaster at Stand Grammar School.

As for the bomb-damaged dwellings that were written off and subsequently demolished, any salvaged metal went towards the manufacture of munitions.

A Reminder

SIX MONTHS AGO GOULBURNS QUOTED THIS VERSE:

"All our past proclaims our future:
Shakespeare's voice and Nelson's hand,
Milton's faith and Wordsworth's trust,
In this our chosen and chainless land,
Bear us witness:
Come the world against her,
England yet shall stand."
                                        —SWINBURNE.

Canned Meals

FOR YOUR

Emergency Cupboards

EXCLUSIVE SPECIALITIES in AMPLE SUPPLY at . . .

GOULBURN'S

GROSVENOR HOTEL (Stockrooms)
MANCHESTER 3

Ask the Hall Porter at the Grosvenor Hotel to direct you to our emergency SHOP and STORE.

Also

27-29-31 EDGE ST. (top of High St.)
MANCHESTER 4

For FISH and other Perishables

(Manchester City News)

The rehousing story – of necessity involved and protracted – is resumed in Chapter Nine. On the subject of repairs, there was one snippet of good news in July:

PUTTING THE BEST FACE ON IT
Holes in the Manchester Town Hall clock face have now been boarded up. The broken glass will not be replaced until after the war.

The holes were caused by bomb blast, which also bent the minute finger of the dial.

(*Manchester Evening News*, 14 July 1941)

In the public domain, there were some successful relocations early that year. The Hallé Orchestra, bombed out of the Free Trade Hall, took up temporary residence in the Odeon cinema on Oxford Street, then in the Opera House. The ruins of the Free Trade Hall were used as a temporary centre for distribution of ration cards to replace those lost in the raids. Arthur Goulburn the mega-grocers, formerly of The Shambles, moved to the basement of the Grosvenor Hotel on Deansgate. The space hitherto used as a bowling alley was now where the cheese was stored. Mr Goulburn enthused about his Stiltons: 'They should have slowly matured for a few weeks after New Year, but the air raid [December 1940] completed the job in a night.' (*Spirit of Manchester*, p. 8.) Timpson's shoe shop on Market Street, gutted in the same Christmas Blitz, reopened for business on the following 11 March, taking over a premises on the opposite side of the street.

In the short term, firms could apply to have their damages in both stock and buildings reimbursed via the national War Damage Commission. Involvement in this plan had been compulsory for all businesses whose property value was at least £50, with a premium of 4s for every £100 of value. For individuals who had losses of small personal possessions whilst engaged in official wartime duties, there was a locally based compensation scheme.

The very fact that a compensation system was not only theoretically in place but also fulfilling its promise for those causes deemed worthy is ample evidence that the city – and indeed national – infrastructure was still operative. Some of the more eye-catching personal claims – all granted by the Emergency Committee – were:

PHILIP HOWARTH (University Warden) 20 Disley Avenue, West Didsbury
Overcoat torn whilst assisting air raid warden

10s

ANNIE O'BRIEN   4 Eden Grove, Manchester 13
Spectacles broken as a result of a blast from an H.E. bomb

16s

SAMUEL BARNETT   20 Lathbury Street, Harpurhey
Raincoat used as stretcher for removal of casualty and enquiries have
since failed to locate the missing article

£1 15s

HENRY COLLINS   3 Brunt Street, Rusholme
Soles of shoes burned while extinguishing an incendiary bomb

6s 6d

JOHN HILL   44 Briscoe Street, Ardwick
Trousers damaged whilst extinguishing incendiary bomb

7s 6d

RICHARD B. ROPER   149 Devon Street, Beswick
Front wheel of bicycle damaged by debris whilst messenger was
performing voluntary duty

6s

Owners of private vehicles damaged whilst performing recognised wartime duties could also apply for compensation, this
time from central government funds. After the December raids
there were fourteen Manchester claimants: four for improvised
ambulances, two for use by wardens, and eight for vehicles used
by the AFS. Claims ranged from £2 13s to £120. The reply from
the Ministry of Home Security in London was that in princi-
ple the government would pay up – but more details would be
required first!

Amongst the AFS personal claims were for seven pairs of spectacles
and two sets of dentures. This perhaps gives some indication of the
age range of many of the fire service volunteers.

Then there was the perennial question of gas masks. After the initial flurry of concern and co-operation, these were increasingly looked upon by the majority of the public as a pointless accessory. It was reported in the *Evening News* in March 1941 that 2,224 gas masks had been left on Manchester buses and trams, most of them minus an identifying label. Other uses had been found for the case, in that, for example, it made a serviceable lunchbox. A lateral-thinking burglar, one Samuel Browne of Chorlton Road, used his mask to smash a draper's window in Old Trafford, before helping himself to an officer's uniform and an ammunition pouch. He received a hefty fine. (More of this sort of thing in the next chapter.)

The government, and by extension Manchester City Council, did its best to persuade people to carry a gas mask at all times. In March 1941, 14,800,000 leaflets – 'What To Do About Gas' – were delivered nationally. The Home Office 'gas van' did the rounds in Manchester, offering free mask tests to anyone who was passing. Regular gas mask exercises were obligatory for schoolchildren, and some firms followed suit. In early summer there was talk of an imminent mock attack in the city centre using tear gas, a prediction given substance by repeated reminders in the newspapers. This turned out to be a partial bluff, in that when the mock attack finally took place (on 31 May) it wasn't in the city centre, but on a basis of voluntary participation in a number of Manchester parks. To some extent it had the desired effect: the Emergency Committee reported a 50 per cent increase in applications for new masks. The cost was 2*s* 9*d*, or 14p: around £7 in today's money.

Possession of a gas mask, however, unlike the blackout, the carrying of ID cards and the new fire-watching regulations, was not enforceable by law.

Stubbornly, Mancunian life carried on. Entertainments were restricted for obvious reasons, and cinema audiences were reported to be 50 per cent down on the usual, with some city-centre theatres reputedly losing as much as £100 a week. Once again ingenuity came to at least a partial rescue. One solution was to reduce prices: the 'Blitz Bargain' came into being. January saw cinemagoers returning in droves to see Chaplin's *The Great Dictator*. Laughing at the thinly disguised Adenoid Hynkel and his cronies Garbitsch and Herring must have been the ideal antidote to the current woes. The film was immensely popular, breaking Manchester box office records, showing simultaneously at three city-centre cinemas, and enjoying a six-week run at the Gaiety. This cinema had recovered from the incendiary raid of the Blitz, replacing the destroyed screen with an improvised one using an old Shakespearean backdrop: a resourceful variation on the 'make do and mend' concept. The traditional seasonal pantomime continued, and the blackout curfew was overcome by shifting the late performance to 11 a.m. or earlier, with great success.

A similar sort of divergent thinking found a highly practical expression with the introduction, in June 1941, of a gas-powered bus. It was the number 53 between Old Trafford and Belle Vue, and although deployed only on a temporary, experimental basis, it went some way towards preserving precious petrol for the war effort.

The air raids, however, were far from finished: on the day after the 8 January public meeting the Luftwaffe launched one of their biggest attacks on Manchester. It lasted six hours, the all-clear sounding at 1.30 a.m. H.E. bombs and incendiaries were scattered across the city, with Blackley and Longsight being the worst-affected residential areas. There were ten fatalities. A gas main was ruptured on the corner of Victoria Avenue and Rochdale Road, creating a major fire which blocked both roads for some time. The north and west of the conurbation received the brunt of the bombing, with Prestwich, Irlam, Swinton, Worsley, Urmston and Trafford Park all being hit. However, by a mixture of good luck and well-organised defensive measures, these areas suffered no casualties, and little damage. German radio was exaggerating the facts when it reported on 10 January: 'In Manchester large numbers of fires were started, some of which, as the night wore on, assumed huge proportions.' This was reported in the *Manchester Evening News* with the defiant headline: 'CAN YOU BELIEVE IT?'

The next significant raid was on 11 March. It lasted three hours, and there were nineteen civilian casualties, mainly in Hulme (Victoria Street and Church Street), Chorlton-on-Medlock, and Chorlton-cum-Hardy. At 19 Torbay Road, Chorlton-cum-Hardy, ARP Warden R.S. Truesdale rescued the Goodyear family, entering the debris several times whilst the bombs were still falling to save Mr Goodyear and his son and two daughters. Sadly the 2-year-old son, Peter, died a short time later, although the rest of the family survived. In Erskine Street, Hulme, a family of four was rescued.

Chorlton-cum-Hardy was hit once more on the night of 1–2 May. Deteriorating weather prompted a recall of Luftwaffe from the Trafford Park area, and bombs were dropped on Egerton Road South and the corner of Cavendish Road (now Corkland Road) and Chatsworth Road. The targets may have been the railway line (now the Metrolink track) or the electricity sub-station on St Werburgh's Road: both were later found highlighted on Luftwaffe maps. The house hit on Egerton Road South belonged to a young couple, the Mooneys, and they had just invested in an interior air-raid shelter, a solid steel construction – the 'Chapman' – designed and installed by a friend. They were playing chess in the shelter when they heard the bomb fall, 'with the biggest smash I have ever heard' according to Mr Mooney. The effectiveness of the shelter – which, unsurprisingly, enjoyed a boost in sales after the story was published in the *Evening News* – may be gauged from the well-known, talismanic photograph which accompanied the report. The photogenic twentysomething couple standing in the ruins of their house and looking remarkably untroubled was an image which served as a powerful confidence-booster. (See Phythian, *South Manchester Remembered*, pp. 85-87.) Significantly, the nine people killed at the same time by a Luftwaffe bomb a couple of hundred yards away received no concurrent publicity. The censorship had a purpose: morale was paramount in 1941.

Maintaining morale was continually a vital factor, and words and images in the public domain played their part. The year 1941 saw the renaming of the LDV (possibly suffering from the jokey 'Look, Duck and Vanish' tag) to the better-equipped Home Guard, which was now reorganised into official battalions. Progressively, the 'Feeding Centres' underwent a revamp and re-emerged as 'British Restaurants'. They operated on a self-service basis, and nearly all building materials used in their construction had been salvaged from blitzed premises. Visits to Manchester from the high-ranking were popular and – after the event, for security reasons – well-publicised: the Duke of Kent in RAF uniform in January, and the king and queen in February. Winston Churchill made a tour of the city in April. (Incidentally, it was February 1945 before Hitler decided to visit a bombed German city.) Popular performers were in demand: in July, Gracie Fields gave concerts at three Manchester munitions factories. Wherever possible, the positive image was sought out and highlighted: in spring 1941 the

Evening News reported that on Ardwick Green, between the rubble of the barracks and the Picturedrome cinema, daffodils were flourishing.

In a typically perverse British way, black humour sometimes helped boost the spirits. One possibly apocryphal story doing the rounds was the following advice on falling bombs from an air-raid warden: 'When you hear a whistle, take shelter. If you hear 'zip-boom' it's dropped. If you hear a harp, your shelter was no good.' (*City News*, 6 December 1940.)

It is but a short step from morale-boosters to jingoism. In March 1941 the right-wing *City News* sacked two conscientious objectors on its staff. Then after the invasion of the Soviet Union the newspaper launched a competition. It was called 'Bombing Back', and with hindsight, it was a shocking trivialisation of the RAF raids, and rather like a small boy pulling faces at his enemy from behind his father's back. There was printed a list of likely targets in Nazi-occupied territory, mostly in France and Germany. Competitors were allowed to place ten crosses alongside the towns or cities they thought were going to be bombed in the next week. The person whose 'pools selection' was closest to the actual raids (at least according to the information received) won 5*s*.

An interesting development throughout 1941 was the increasing virtual presence of the USA in Britain. Although supposedly neutral, the States had supplied Britain, via the 'Lease-Lend' agreement, a considerable quota of war equipment. Well before Pearl Harbor, US support for the Allied cause was in evidence, and there were echoes of this in Manchester. The aforementioned film *Manchester Took It, Too* has a short section featuring Wendell Willkie, the US businessman and politician who, although a Republican, had stated his firm support for Roosevelt the Democrat President in the matter of the European War. Willkie saw the military sense in hoping Britain did not succumb to the Nazis, thereby losing the Atlantic Ocean as a buffer zone. It made economic sense too: the rigid central control of the Fascist economies would not interact well with the entrepreneurial policies of the Land of Opportunity. The scene in the film shows Willkie visiting bomb-sites and meeting the people of Manchester. ('An autograph? Sure. Now where's that fountain pen?' narrates the voice-over.)

American support came to Manchester in other forms. The mayor, Alderman R.G. Edwards, received a cheque for $1,500 from a Mr Morris Haft, who had been to primary school in Manchester

BOMB
with the R.A.F.

MAP OUT OPERATIONS AND WIN A PRIZE

("City News" Copyright.)

Our competition has caught the imagination in several quarters, and probably there are other offices like that of the "City News" (members of our staff are not allowed to compete) where employes are filling up the forms and having a friendly competition amongst themselves.

The winner of Contest No. 1 will be announced next Friday.

One competitor, we notice, has placed three crosses against a certain objective. We asked you to place two crosses if you anticipate a place being bombed more than once . You have the liberty of putting three crosses if you wish, but of course, it is increasing your task of having an all-correct forecast.

The rules once again. Select your own objectives likely to be visited by the R.A.F. bombers during a period of seven days, which means you can add your own fancy to the list we publish. You have ten bombs to drop and have to try to anticipate the places to be visited by our Bombers—for this Contest No. 3—during the week August 7 to 13 inclusive. Official communiques are used as the basis for judging the winner.

MUNSTER.	FRANKFURT.
DUSSELDORF.	COLOGNE.
BREST.	WILHELMSHAVEN.
BOLOGNE.	BREMEN.
KIEL.	BERLIN.
ESSEN.	HAMBURG.
LORIENT.	HAMM.
OSNABRUCK.	DORTMUND.
DUISBURG.	MANNHEIM.

Name ....

Address ....

....

Address your entry to: "Bombing Back," No. 3, "CITY NEWS," 119, Corn Exchange Buildings, Manchester, 4, to be received before Wednesday, August 6th.

(Manchester City News)

along with his four brothers, and no doubt had positive memories of his time there. The money was to be put towards a mobile feeding station. Another mobile canteen was donated by the firm of Compton and Knowles of Worcester, Massachusetts. The Oregon branch of the campaign of 'bundles for Britain' raised £123, and a Beverley Hills swimming gala raised 'over 500 guineas' for the 'Manchester Distress Fund'. (Details from *MEN*, June 1941.)

Food parcels arrived from the USA, containing non-perishable goods such as dried and tinned fruit, and powdered egg and potato. The British diet was also introduced to tins of reconstituted meat known as Spam. The *New York Times* announced that 'American aid to Britain has increased from a trickle to an ever broadening stream'.

Naturally the Commonwealth helped out too. New Zealand sent butter, cheese and wool, and according to the *MEN* of 9 July 1941, 'seven times more wheat than the weight of the liner *Queen Elizabeth*'. Significantly, bread was never subject to rationing. Closer to home the Isle of Man supplied eggs (real ones), kippers and tomatoes. More mobile canteens were donated by Trinidad and Tobago and Southern Rhodesia.

The raids had continued throughout early summer. On the night of 7–8 May there were a number of casualties in the Higher Broughton and Pendleton districts of Salford, whilst in Stretford there were injuries and fatalities reported in Skelton Road and Audley Avenue. On the same night Meadow Street and Darncombe Street in Moss Side and Whitchurch Road in Withington were badly damaged. The blast hit Alexandra Road South, where the English Martyrs' church lost some of its stained-glass windows, renowned as amongst the most beautiful in the city.

In Moss Side, Heywood Street ran north–south, parallel to Meadow Street on the opposite side of Alexandra Road. Several houses on this street were demolished, including No. 34, where during the night cries for help were heard coming from the cellar. An 18-stone woman was trapped by rubble, and water from a ruptured water main was rapidly filling the cellar. Two pumps were put to work, but the water was rising faster than both of them could cope with. Working partly under water for over an hour and a half, the rescue squad managed to locate the blocks of debris and eventually freed the woman, who suffered only minor injuries.

There was a heartening coda to this raid – perhaps indicative of the way the tide was slowly turning – which was made a lot of by the local press. At around 1.15 a.m. a Heinkel 111 was shot down by a Defiant night fighter and crash-landed on what is now Stockport Golf Course (then Torkington Golf Links). Eyewitness Kenneth Shepley was in the back garden of his parents' house off Marple Road, Offerton, when the incident occurred:

> I was watching shell bursts when I saw a bright light coming towards us from the Hazel Grove area. It seemed to get brighter and lower in the sky.
>
> I then realised it was a plane on fire.
>
> I thought it was going to drop on top of us, but over Beanleach Road it seemed to veer to the right and I thought it had come down behind Mr Bugby's farm, a little further up Marple Road.
>
> (*Manchester Evening News* Correspondence, 27 August 1980)

Darncombe Street in Moss Side after the 7 May 1940 raid. This was near to the present-day Brentwood Street. *(Greater Manchester Police Museum and Archives)*

The four-man crew had parachuted out of the stricken plane, and all four were captured in various districts of south Stockport. One landed on a Bramhall rooftop, another in a Cheadle street, and another in a playing field near the Mirrlees factory, also in Bramhall. The fourth member of the crew only just managed to bale out in time, and so landed a few hundred yards from where the plane hit the ground with a huge explosion.

There was a massive raid on Manchester on the night of 1–2 June. The 1 June was Whit Sunday, again demonstrating the Luftwaffe's liking for attacks at or near holiday time. Apart from the two Christmas attacks the previous year, this was the most intense bombing experienced by the city. Its ferocity had a strategic purpose beyond the obvious, as it helped to smoke-screen Hitler's real intention for summer 1941: the invasion of the Soviet Union. There were to be no more major air raids on Manchester after this one, as most German resources were now being poured into Operation Barbarossa.

Central Manchester took another hammering. There were nearly fifty casualties, mainly from the Cheetham and Crumpsall areas. The Assize Courts at Strangeways, mostly spared in the Christmas Blitz, was now reduced to rubble, with just the ornate front facade left standing. Over 2,000 rare antique law books valued at £10,000 were lost in the bombing. Peter Street was hit, with damage to the Theatre Royal and the Gaiety, the Café Royal and the YMCA building. The Bootle Street Police HQ had its upper floors wrecked and two Civil Defence messengers were killed, but police work nevertheless continued.

In an attempt to ignore the devastation, Mancunians were determined to enjoy the Whit holiday weekend as best they could. Belle Vue was as usual the fun-seekers' magnet, advertising the switchback ride on The Bobs, animal rides, speedway and wrestling. ('Come smiling through' said the poster.) Fairey's Aviation Works Band gave a concert there on the Sunday evening. In the city centre, the surviving cinemas were running a full programme: the News Theatre was showing a 'Whit Week Whoopee' which featured some Chaplin shorts and 'the latest Popeye'. Arthur Askey was starring in *Ghost Train* at the Gaumont, whilst Henry Fonda and Dorothy Lamour were in the circus melodrama *Chad Hanna* at the Odeon. The Burnage annual gala went ahead as planned at the cricket club, but minus the usual coconut shy, as the target coconuts proved impossible to obtain.

People were advised to stay at home to avoid putting extra pressure on the railways, but Blackpool was as always a popular destination for Manchester trippers. However, the dense crowds and long queues detracted considerably from the famous fresh air and fun. As one person put it: 'Some holiday this! I wish I'd stayed at home and had a rest. I shall need another holiday to recover from the strain of the last few days.' (*Manchester Evening News*, 2 June 1941.)

There was one further attack that year: on the night of 12–13 October, Bank Street in Clayton and Homerton Road in Newton Heath were hit, with three casualties. Oldham received the worst of it that night, with twenty-seven fatalities. The all-clear sounded at 1 a.m., less than two hours after the initial warning siren.

Despite the near total absence of air raids during the second half of the year, official complacency was taboo. Following on from the mock gas attack in May, the Civil Defence authorities staged a much-publicised simulated invasion of Manchester at dawn on Sunday, 26 October 1941. The *City News* had advised, two days before: 'The public are warned to carry both gas masks and ID cards, as well as to be prepared for much noise from thunder flashes and dive-bombing aeroplanes in some localities … Traffic delays may occur, and motorists are warned that they may find petrol stations immobilised.'

The actual 'invasion' was considerably more low-key. A bunch of pretend fifth columnists disrupted traffic with a STOP/GO sign in Albert Square, and some disguised infiltrators tried to take over the BBC building in Piccadilly. In both cases the Home Guard unmasked the perpetrators, in one instance almost literally, by pulling the wig off the head of a female impersonator. The object of the exercise, according to General Sir Robert Gordon Finlayson, had been to 'test arrangements for co-operation between civil and military defence forces'. Lines of communication were shown to be in splendid trim, and 'the spirit of the Home Guard was excellent'.

In the global context, 1941 ended with an escalation of the war. Pearl Harbor brought the Americans into the European and Asian battlegrounds, meaning that people were no longer pondering over whether to call the conflict 'The Second German War' or 'The Second European War'. For the second time in a generation, in one way or another virtually the whole world would henceforth be involved.

In Manchester, the year ended on a note of near-farce. On Christmas Eve, with Market Street full of shoppers, without warning two bombers suddenly appeared overhead. As the bomb doors opened memories of the previous Christmas Blitz caused some measure of panic in the streets below, and one person was knocked down by a slow-moving car. Apart from this, there were no injuries or casualties, as the planes were British Whitney bombers, and the bomb load was 10,000 leaflets from the city police, wishing everyone a Merry Christmas, and reminding people of the benefits of road safety. Lord Mayor Alderman Wright Robinson commented: 'I am sure it was well meant, but might have been more fortunately planned.' It was a very rare example of a lack of official foresight in Manchester during those years.

WHAT TO DO BEFORE GOING TO YOUR SHELTER

-and the help that is ready if your home is hit

...ave the all gas ...ot jets, e main. ...water ...front. ...e the ...amp, ...can ...cur- ...pper ...hich ...ible ...ay

Bottle of water, and to drink out of. Sli clean stockings or case your feet get going to shelter). Knitting or some kind to do. Something t Ear plugs. Keep something to eat you, in case you get pec the night. Hot drinks can be kept warm by wrapping in a bl though a 'hay - bottl better. Instructions for m a 'hay-bottle' are conta (with many other useful h ...ir very helpful leaflets b issued to all who sleep shelters.

AFTER THE RAIL

Have your plans made

Make plans now to go and stay with friends living near, but not too near, in case your house is destroyed. They should also arrange now to come to you if their house is knocked out. It's comforting to feel that every- thing is fixed up, just in case.

Help is ready

If your house is damaged, there is a great deal of help ready for you. Full arrangements have been made to give you food and shelter, clothes and money if necessary and to find you some- where to live. If you have not been able to make arrangements with friends, go straight to the emergency Rest Centre. The wardens and police know where is. *Ask them.*

SEVEN

'GET WHAT YOU CAN': UNDER THE COVER OF DARKNESS

- A LOOK AT LIFE IN THE SHELTERS AND THE BLACKOUT •
- SHELTERS CLEAN-UP •
- LOOTING, SCAMS, BLACK MARKET AND OTHER PERIPHERAL ACTIVITIES •
- CENSORSHIP, LORD HAW-HAW AND THE MISINFORMATION WAR •

We have seen plenty of evidence to support the view that war brings out the best in people; unfortunately, it can also bring out the worst.

Numerous examples of this ambivalence may be found in reports of what went on in communal air-raid shelters during the Manchester Blitz. On the plus side there was the courage and community spirit brought about by the common enemy. There were also the facilities – some of them quite sophisticated, like organised activities, hot drink sales and even small libraries – available in some of the larger shelters. On the debit side there was reported anti-social behaviour ranging from the irritating to the blatantly criminal. One has to have sympathy, though, with 53-year-old George Hall, sentenced to two weeks in prison in December 1941. His crime? Snoring too loudly whilst asleep in a public shelter.

A couple of contrasting viewpoints, both from early on in the Luftwaffe raids, will help to set the scene. Councillor Harper, chief ARP warden for the city centre, had this to say:

> On the whole, the public are well-behaved, though there have been isolated cases of week-end disturbances, drunkenness and fighting. A soldier the other night settled an argument by clouting a drunken man over the earhole. That was taking the law into his own hands, but it was effective.
>
> (*Manchester Evening News*, 20 September 1940)

This was perhaps the guarded, partly conciliatory view of a politician. The Reverend Peter Green (whom we met briefly in Chapter One) would not have agreed with Councillor Harper:

> Cases have been instanced of drunken women as well as men causing trouble; of bands of young hooligans who sit up singing bawdy songs and swearing; the domestic quarrels caused by drunkenness, and of sober men and women who have risked death or injury by leaving rowdy shelters and going elsewhere for quiet … Young men with accordions and mouth organs also cause complaint.
>
> (*Manchester City News*, 12 September 1940)

The question of singing in shelters seemed to divide general opinion. Initially the council had recommended it as a way of keeping a brave face on things. But in reality it was like alcohol: in reasonable volume and measure, well-blended, and following a communally acceptable menu, it could be inspiring. Too much of the wrong stuff, though, tended to cause disruption. What constituted the 'wrong stuff' was sometimes the subject of fervent debate. A correspondent calling himself 'Freedom' had this to relate:

> While the sirens were sounding one night I went into a public air raid shelter in Failsworth. The warden advised us to sing, and we began singing all the latest dance hits. About 10 minutes later a police sergeant and a constable came in and told us that if we did not stop singing we would all have to leave.
>
> (*Manchester City News* Correspondence, 13 June 1941)

BEFORE, DURING AND AFTER THE RAID

WHAT TO DO BEFORE GOING TO YOUR SHELTER

—and the help that is ready if your home is hit

BEFORE you leave the house, turn off all gas taps, including pilot jets, and turn off the gas at the main. Leave buckets or cans of water and sand or earth on the front-door step, or just inside the door. Put your stirrup pump, if you have one, where it can easily be seen. Draw back curtains and raise blinds in upper rooms so that any fires which may be started may be visible from the outside. This may save your house.

CLOTHING

Dress yourself and your children (particularly your children) warmly before leaving the house, even if the shelter is close by. You will be going from the warm house into the cold night air, and it will take a little time before you are settled down and in bed, and you should not risk anyone getting chilled before getting into bed. Also, if anything happens to your house during the night, or you should have to leave your shelter, you will have something warm to put on.

WHAT TO TAKE WITH YOU

Your money and any valuables or documents, such as rent book, or building society book, insurance policy, records of instalment payments, shaded torch, Gas Mask, Identity Card, Ration Book, etc.

Bottle of water, and something to drink out of. Slippers and clean stockings or socks (in case your feet get wet when going to shelter).
Knitting or some kind of work to do. Something to read.
Ear plugs.
Keep something to eat beside you, in case you get peckish in the night.
Hot drinks can be kept fairly warm by wrapping in a blanket, though a 'hay-bottle' is better. Instructions for making a 'hay-bottle' are contained (with many other useful hints) in very helpful leaflets being issued to all who sleep in shelters.

AFTER THE RAID

Have your plans made

Make plans now to go and stay with friends living near, but not too near, in case your house is destroyed. They should also arrange now to come to you if their house is knocked out. It's comforting to feel that everything is fixed up, just in case.

Help is ready

If your home is damaged, there is a great deal of help ready for you. Full arrangements have been made to give you food and shelter, clothes and money if necessary and to find you somewhere to live. If you have not been able to make arrangements with friends, go straight to the emergency Rest Centre. The wardens and police know where it is. *Ask them.*

ISSUED BY THE MINISTRY OF HOME SECURITY

(Manchester Evening News)

An argument ensued, and the writer, after being threatened with expulsion from the shelter, concluded that the officers of the law were 'carrying officialdom a little too far'.

The happy alternative was in evidence when a choir had to abandon a concert in the Albert Hall on Peter Street and take refuge in the Manchester and Salford Junction Canal tunnel below Deansgate:

> ... in a little while the great shelter was echoing with the sound of carols and favourite hymns. Some of the regular occupants joined in too. ... At times we could hear the roar of the guns and the thud of the bombs from the nightmare world above, but we sang on until we were too tired to produce another note.
>
> (*Spirit of Manchester*, p. 8)

It has to be said that conditions in the public shelters were initially poor. Overcrowded, badly ventilated, with scant seating and inadequate toilet facilities, they were high on the Emergency Committee's agenda for the New Year 1941. The principal fault had been one of conception: originally the shelters were intended only for raids of two to three hours at most. Nobody had considered the possibility of all-night bombings, with people being forced to stay in a cramped, smelly bunker with limited toilet facilities for twelve to fifteen hours at a stretch.

Conditions in some shelters were so bad that there was sometimes an exodus to the nearest Rest Centre, thus putting even more pressure on those premises which were supposed to act as a temporary haven for those bombed out of their home. A case in point was the Zion Centre on Stretford Road, Hulme. The basement had been divided into two sections: the air-raid shelter and the Rest Centre, separated by a locked door. The shelter had been intended for 200 people, but on one occasion during the raids 800 were crammed into it. The Emergency Committee minutes for 15 January 1941 record that the communicating door was broken down, and the crowd 'overwhelmed' the Rest Centre staff.

One major worry was the potential for spreading disease in the crowded and poorly ventilated shelters. There was a scarlet fever scare early in 1941, and concern was expressed about outbreaks of diphtheria, scabies, whooping cough, and pneumonia. It was felt that bacteria were being spread by sneezing and coughing in the enclosed space. (The public announcement *Coughs and sneezes spread diseases – trap the germs in your handkerchief!* a strident version of which was still being televised in the sixties, had its origins in the Blitz.) The *City News* reported that the medical journal *The Lancet* had published an article on the danger of 'shelter legs'. This complaint, apparently, was caused by prolonged pressure from the wooden crossbar of a deck-chair on the popliteal muscle (that's the one at the back of the knee, to me and you). However, the censor seems to have exerted his influ-ence again, since the title of the original *Lancet* article was 'Shelter deaths from pulmonary embolism'. In any case, deckchairs were soon replaced by two- or three-tier bunks.

Ivy Forth of Woollam Place, off Liverpool Road, had this to say about the Manchester and Salford Junction Canal (MSJC) tunnel shelter, early on in the war: 'It was the biggest and safest shelter in Manchester, but it was running with water and it was terrible! There were beds of all kinds – it was like a doss house! People from all round Manchester took their beds down there.' (*The Manchester Village: Deansgate Remembered*, p. 54.)

V. Lloyd, who used to travel to the shelter from Hulme with his family, described it as 'cold, black, and damp, but a second home to us … a life-saver' (*MEN* Correspondence, 9 March 2002). On top of the existing health hazards, some of the shelters were even being used for fly-tipping. Clearly a significant rethink and overhaul was needed.

Royal physician Lord Horder went on a tour of inspection of public shelters and published the results of his findings in the pam-phlet *Conditions in Air Raid Shelters* in January 1941. He was none too impressed by what he had found. The following recommenda-tions were made:

Bunks, lighting and sanitary arrangements
First-aid posts
Heating and ventilation
Use of spray antibacterial disinfectant, such as sodium hypochlorite
Face masks to minimise spread of infection by coughing and sneezing
Inoculation against diphtheria to be encouraged

Manchester took the improvements several stages further. To take the MSJC tunnel as an example, by October 1941 the significant overhaul had included: the closing of the most insanitary sections; a temporary steel roof to drain off the dripping water; a first-aid point with trained nurses; a total of 585 seats and 783 bunks; heating, usually by slow-combustion stoves, although electric heating was given a trial run later; a rudimentary, but successful, air-conditioning system run by four generators; a ticket system so that the local people could always gain entry; more toilets with proper plumbing; a kitchen and several boilers; hot and cold water in washbasins, and drinking fountains; daily disinfection and removal of bedding; and a sales point which supplied refreshments and hot drinks (the crockery was shared with the Victoria Arches shelters). By late summer 1941 the Manchester and Salford Methodist Mission was conducting a Sunday evening service in the tunnel. Sales of hot drinks proved immensely popular: the Emergency Committee minuted that in one week in April 1942, 438 cups of tea, Oxo or cocoa had been sold, creating a profit for the week of 3s 2d! Between June 1942 and May 1943 – by which time, of course, the bombings were all but over – no fewer than 25,203 cups of tea were sold.

The Victoria Arches had undergone a similar transformation. By August 1942 they had seating space for 1,016, and 603 bunks. Maximum emergency capacity was given as 5,600, but only if the ventilation system was working. By then it was estimated that Manchester had 381 basement shelters, with a capacity of over 60,000, and thanks to a good deal of voluntary work, conditions had improved in all of them. Some of them even had libraries of donated books and children's comics, although for some reason – possibly the potential fire risk – the idea was none too popular with the Emergency Committee.

As conditions took a turn for the better, so concern shifted to shelters being used for purposes not envisaged by the Civil Defence. Four Rusholme men were caught playing a game of solo whist for money, well after the 'raiders past' siren had otherwise emptied the shelter. Since unlicensed gambling in a public place was illegal, the droll summing-up from the judge at their trial went: 'If you had not been playing solo you might not have gone misère this morning. You will each be fined twenty shillings.' (*Manchester Evening News*, 24 October 1940.)

Courting couples used the empty shelters if they wanted a bit of privacy. On the shady side, ladies of the night began using them to ply their trade. As often, awareness of this practice found its way into popular culture. A music hall song going the rounds – a masterpiece of double entendre when performed by Florence Desmond – was 'The Deepest Shelter in Town'. (Fred Wedlock borrowed the tune for his 1981 hit 'The Oldest Swinger in Town'.) A few sample verses:

Don't run away, mister,
Oh stay and play, mister.
Don't worry if you hear the siren go.
Though I'm not a lady of the highest virtue,
I wouldn't dream of letting anything hurt you.
And so before you go,
I think you ought to know
… I've got the deepest shelter in town.

I've got a cosy flat,
There's a place for your hat,
I'll wear a pink chiffon negligée gown.
And do I know my stuff?
But if that's not enough
I've got the deepest shelter in town.

Every modern comfort
I can just guarantee.
If you hear the siren call
Then it's probably me.

There were many suggestions for legal and socially acceptable enter-
tainment to help pass the time, take the mind off the bombing,
and generally improve behaviour. The Editorial of the *City News* gave
the following recommendations (touching once more on the issue
of singing): 'A competent person with a concertina, and one or two
people with good voices, or somebody who can keep people inter-
ested in guessing-game sort of amusements, might be worth a good
many clerical collars … or policemen's helmets.' (*Manchester City
News*, 12 September 1940.)

Reverend R.G. Myers wrote to the *Guardian* in April 1941, taking
pride in the fact that under the Oxford Hall on Oxford Road the
shelter of which he was in charge put on 'musical evenings, community singing … films, travel talks, and lantern lectures'.

Those with a good memory were sometimes asked to recite a
favourite poem, although the Gorton shelter that was subjected to
a Mr Wimbury's declamation of 'The Green Eye of the Little Yellow
God' nearly every night might possibly have found it wearing thin
after a while. (See *Manchester at War: The People's Story*, p. 63.)

Life in the air-raid shelters cannot be reduced to one umbrella description: like life on the surface, it was the best of times and the worst of times – and most of the possibilities in between – depending on the conditions, the occupants, the person(s) in charge, and the proximity of the bombs.

There is no doubt that criminal activity increased during and after the Blitz (apart from shoplifting, which actually decreased in Manchester, perhaps because there were fewer goods on display due to the Limitation of Supplies Order). With most of the police force busy elsewhere, with rationing providing a golden opportunity for the profiteers, and with the blackout covering a multitude of sins, the criminal, both petty and big time, came into his own.

There were also the many new rules and regulations which caught out the generally law-abiding. Harry Atkins of Withington was fined 10s in January 1941 for taking photos of damaged buildings, even though the judge conceded that 'the law was broken innocently'. In June of the same year Francis James Stewart, a 25 year old from Oldham, accidentally rang the bell of Corpus Christi church in Chadderton. Since church bells were of necessity kept silent during the war years, to be rung only in the event of invasion, the slip of the hand was severely punished, and Stewart was sent to prison for a month.

Less innocent were the shopkeepers who overpriced their food – oranges and eggs especially. There was an agreed price for every item of food, and a shopkeeper was breaking the law if he charged more.

The black market was rife, ranging from the neighbourhood butcher who slipped an extra sausage into a favoured customer's order, to the supposedly nationwide criminal syndicate. This latter came to Mancunian public attention in early summer of 1941, when over 5 tons of bacon disappeared from an abandoned lorry in the Manchester area. The police made an intensive search of likely hiding places, warning that they had a 'list of receivers' who were being watched. The *Evening News* reported that the police had been informed of the markings on the bacon. It was never found, and neither were the 7 million cigarettes stolen from a goods train in Mottram on 11 June. The theory was expressed that behind all the large thefts there was a London-based organisation running the black market on a national scale. Whether this organisation existed or not is difficult to prove either way, but it made good copy.

A typical ration book. The laws for use were necessarily stringent. *(Philip Lloyd)*

Other minor breaches of regulations included selling unwanted ration coupons to friends for cash, and the arrangement between employees of the adjacent firms Hedley & Co. Ltd and Corn Products Co. Ltd in Trafford Park, whereby rationed items sugar and cooking fat were exchanged by throwing them over the adjoining wall during the night shift.

Numerous minor scams were reported. Two workers from Gorton were employed to shift some timber from a bombed area, for re-use by the council. They kept some of it for themselves, selling it on at £2 a load. This turned out to be unprofitable, as they were found out, and fined £6 each. A little further down the road to perdition, six men in New Moston who were employed to reinforce some Anderson shelters with cement stole some and did a 'foreigner', building some paths for private houses. Their fine was £4 each.

False compensation claims rarely succeeded because of the rigorous verification process, and penalties for would-be fraudsters were harsh. A James Duffy claimed £6 for his allegedly blitzed stepfather's business premises in Upper Lloyd Street, Hulme. A check revealed that the premises were actually undamaged, and Duffy was jailed for three months. Lilian Downing of Ogden Street, Old Trafford, made bogus claims for blitzed furniture at addresses at which she had never lived. The judge commented that such crimes were 'helping the enemy', which seemed to justify the three months' jail sentence. Five years' imprisonment was the sentence passed on another claimant, who went so far as to lie about the death of members of his family. No Mancunian had as much barefaced cheek as Londoner Walter Handy, though, who claimed to have been bombed out nineteen times in five months. When the repeated fraud was finally discovered he was sent to jail for three years.

A number of fire-watchers took advantage of the empty premises they were supposed to be guarding to make off with some of the goods. Fines for such thefts were surprisingly low – usually around £2 – compared with the hefty penalties for breach of blackout and food price regulations, which ranged from £4 to £15 (around £200 to £750 in today's money), or even a prison sentence. For example, a Prestwich grocer sold a 1s tin of plums for 1s 3d, and was fined £4. A Salford butcher was found guilty of overcharging, and was sent to jail for twenty-one days.

The darkness of the blackout was a boon to the petty criminal. The *Manchester Guardian* of 4 May 1942 said as much, quoting Chief Constable Sir John Maxwell. Even before the war started, the absence of street lighting had been exploited. During the practice blackout of 31 March–1 April 1939, a youth and a boy were seen on Liverpool Road carrying a cigarette machine they'd just removed from a wall outside a shop. At about the same time a man had been arrested in Leigh for breaking into a school 'with intent to steal'. During the war itself crimes on the increase were theft of bicycles, housebreaking and larceny, and false pretences and fraud. Most lucrative illegal activities were the stealing and selling on of petrol, ration books, and restricted foodstuffs, crimes which proved difficult to track down. Theft of petrol from Red Cross vehicles was prevented by inserting a spiral spring device in the neck of the tank, which made it impossible to insert a siphon. Also, petrol for official use was dyed pink, which made it much easier to trace.

How widespread was looting from bombed premises in Manchester? It is difficult to say exactly. A headline from the *MEN* (9 January 1941) was unequivocal: 'Looting Becoming Serious in Manchester, Court Told.'

On the other hand, Herbert Morrison, speaking in the Commons later in the year, tried to play things down: 'My information does not support the suggestion that there is a considerable increase in the number of cases of looting.' (Hansard, 1 May 1941.)

This of course does not deny that looting was taking place, even though few specific cases made it as far as the newspapers. This policy made sense, since if the German High Command had caught a whiff of social collapse it would have been a propaganda godsend, and the bombing would conceivably have been stepped up. The *Manchester Guardian* reported in October 1947 that throughout the war there had been 5,000 cases of looting found proven in magistrates' courts in England and Wales. Leeds Assizes spent over two whole days in December 1940 trying looters from Sheffield, imposing custodial sentences totalling 38½ years. There is no reason to suppose that Manchester was an oasis of innocent non-participation.

One instance of looting that was recorded in the *Evening News* concerned a Stretford man who entered a bomb-damaged pub and helped himself to a cash register containing £4 10s. When police found the till in his outhouse, his excuse was that he hadn't really stolen it, but was 'preserving the property' and 'minding it for the licensee'. Another instance of the looter using bogus altruism as a pretext was a 17-year-old who was found helping himself to the goods in a blitzed shoe shop on Market Street. He asked the man who discovered him, 'Do you want to buy a pair of shoes?' Unfortunately this person turned out to be a magistrate, who handed the young man over to the police. In court the accused posed the question: 'Should it be right that shoes should be left there while there are people walking about without them?' Needless to say, this cut no ice with the judge. (*Manchester Evening Chronicle*, 18 January 1941.)

Meanwhile, the more sensational newspapers seethed with moral outrage. The *Daily Mirror* in November 1940 blared: 'Hang a looter and stop this filthy crime!' This seems to have overlooked the fact that a significant number of the city pilferers were children. With most parents involved in demanding war work of one kind or another, children were quite often left to their own devices, unsupervised. Roy Hill was a 12 year old at the time of the Manchester Christmas Blitz. He relates that after a raid his best friend was buried under some rubble. Roy was present during the four-hour rescue attempt, and he remembers people digging and throwing bricks to one side. He recalls his friend's remains being found, and that was when he believes something snapped: 'I just thought, "Well, what's the use?" He was dead. If I was going to live, I wanted more than he had – live for today. Get what you can.' (*Bad Boys of the Blitz*: Channel Five, 3 May 2007.)

He started taking things from bombed houses, reasoning that if he didn't help himself, somebody else would. Police records reveal a sharp rise in juvenile crime from 1940 to 1941: for example, the figures for Salford show a 75 per cent increase. Young children were involved in pilfering, sometimes for themselves, sometimes as part of a larger adult scheme. In Burnage a man and woman sent out a gang of children to local farms to steal poultry, and a man was jailed for receiving stolen goods from a 10-year-old boy. A woman was sent to prison for organising house burglaries by two boys aged 12. This Fagin-style arrangement accounted for 5 per cent of all juvenile crime in Manchester in 1941. One striking statistic was the escalation in crime among young girls, for whom the crime of breaking and entering tripled during the war years. (*Manchester Guardian*, 21 October 1947.)

The problems were exacerbated by the fact that many child evacuees had returned to the city as a result of the false calm of the phoney war. The *City News* reported that by mid-December 1940, out of the original 20,000 children billeted elsewhere the previous Christmas, only 5,000 remained in their adopted homes. In some cases, this return continued even after the bombing had started. In January 1941 two Old Trafford brothers, aged 12 and 10, came back from their billet in Bury without their parents' knowledge. Fearing punishment if they went back home, they stole a few shillings from a shop, and were discovered sleeping out in the deserted Trafford cinema.

One bit of thieving by a youngster had a tragic outcome. In June 1941, 18-year-old Hugh Baxter of Monton stole an automatic gun from the Eccles War Weapons Week at Brotherhood Hall. He unscrewed the metal staples holding the gun in place and made off with the weapon hidden under his coat. Whilst he was showing it to friends in the garden shed later that day, the gun went off, fatally wounding him.

It must be stressed that the bad boys (and girls) featuring in this chapter were very much in the minority. Ian Meadowcroft relates that as a child in Whalley Range he went round bombed houses with a group of friends, but they did nothing wilder than play hide and seek, avoiding the shakier-looking parts of what remained of the structure. Most of the youngsters who were able helped out with fire-watching or dousing incendiaries, and those with bicycles became ARP messengers. The *City News* recorded in September 1941 that over 1,300 boys aged 16 or over had volunteered for the messenger service. Special Scout and Civil awards were bestowed on under-18s mentioned in dispatches, as it were, and most of the schoolchildren of Manchester were involved to some extent with fund-raising.

Unsurprisingly, for reasons of morale newspapers tended to emphasise the positive and play down or ignore the negative. Censorship was therefore strict, with many of the dispiriting stories and photographs not making it to the public domain, sometimes for months or even years to come. As a councillor put it, in March 1941: 'If you want to know nothing, ask the Chief Constable.'

The information war was ever in full spate. Gordon Banner, organist at the Odeon Theatre, penned the following, to be sung to the old standard 'Somewhere a Voice is Calling':

> *Somewhere a voice is calling*
> *O'er Germany*
> *Butting in Nazi broadcasts,*
> *Who can it be?*
>
> *When they announce their losses*
> *Guess their surprise*
> *Somewhere that 'voice' comes calling:*
> *Lies, Nazi lies.*

(*Manchester City News*, 12 September 1941)

Early on in the war, there was an ironic twist to the usually accepted scenario: during the first couple of years of hostilities there was often more truth in Lord Haw-Haw's propaganda radio broadcasts from Hamburg than there was in the official British news.

Alan Eachus remembers Lord Haw-Haw appearing to show an unnervingly precise knowledge of Manchester streets. In one broadcast he specified 'the people in Brunswick Street' in Ardwick as a target. This was shortly before the nearby Drill Hall on Ardwick Green was bombed. Sandra Parker's uncle, Clifford Frith, was a prisoner of war when Lord Haw-Haw announced: 'Mr and Mrs Frith we have your son, Clifford, and we know you live near the viaducts in Stockport. We are coming to bomb your houses.' Another boast was: 'We know where the gasometers are in Hyde, and we will bomb them.' Salford wasn't spared the scaremongering: 'We are going to make Irwell Valley a valley of death, and the Irwell a river of blood.' Eve O'Neill recalls him saying that the Luftwaffe pilots knew where the Fairey Aviation factory was, near to McVitie's in Heaton Chapel: the final word, for some reason, was pronounced – incorrectly and pretentiously – with the accent on the second syllable.

By the end of the war, however, Lord Haw-Haw had become a figure of fun, much parodied, the Comical Ali of his day. The man behind the patronising upper-class voice, William Joyce, an Oldham man and ex-member of Mosley's Fascists, was hanged for treason in January 1946.

The final conventional bombing raid on Manchester took place around 8 a.m. on 27 July 1942. A lone Junkers dropped a stick of bombs on Ancoats and Beswick, causing considerable damage to Palmerston Street, Hillkirk Street, and Russell Street. Possibly the target was Ancoats Goods Station, which was on the site of what is now the Piccadilly Trading Estate, off Great Ancoats Street. The alert lasted just seventeen minutes, but the attack left three dead and seven seriously injured. After this, Manchester was free of attacks for nearly two and a half years.

The Emergency Committee held its last regular monthly meeting in July 1944. Full blackout restrictions were lifted throughout England (apart from on the east coast) in September. By the end of that year, with the Allies cutting deep into former occupied territory in Europe, Mancunians were convinced that as far as they were concerned Nazi Germany – despite the V-1 and V-2 attacks on London and the Home Counties – was a spent force, and that raids on the north-west of England were very much a thing of the past. They were confident that they were out of range of the flying bombs. On Christmas Eve 1944 they were proven wrong.

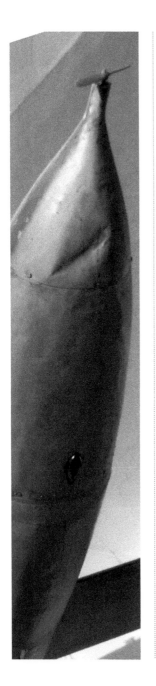

EIGHT

'A DULL, PULSATING ROAR': THE NIGHT OF THE DOODLEBUGS

● CHRISTMAS EVE 1944: OLDHAM, WORSLEY, HYDE, STOCKPORT AND DIDSBURY HIT BY V-1S ●

Towards the end of the war Hitler made repeated references to a new and terrible weapon which would dramatically reverse Germany's fortunes and bring the rest of the world to heel. How close the Nazis were to creating an atom bomb could be the subject of an entire book, and is outside the scope of this one. Leaving speculation aside, the 'revenge weapon' developed at Peenemünde and unleashed on Britain in 1944 was frightening enough. The pilotless or robot bomb must have seemed like something out of science fiction.

The technology of the *Vergeltungswaffe1* was still very much in the experimental stage. This explains why actual impact points were wildly erratic, and why there were so many accidents on launching. The specifications of the V-1 flying bomb were:

Length:	7.7m (25ft 4in)
Wingspan:	5.3m (17ft 4in)
Explosive weight:	850kg (1,870lb)
Overall weight:	2,180kg (4,800lb)
Maximum speed:	654km/h (400mph)
Range:	265km (165 miles)

The range would be increased later to 400km (250 miles) with the introduction of wooden wings and reduced explosive load. This still meant
that the North of England was well out of range of V-1s launched from
static sites. By December 1944 the only launch sites available to the

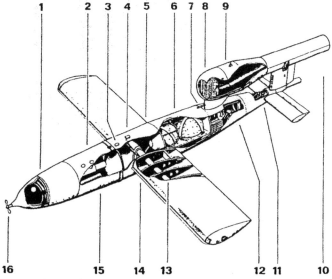

Internal details of a Type 1 Flying Bomb. **Key: 1.** Compass to control gyros
for guidance, enclosed in non-magnetic (wooden) sphere; **2.** twin fuse
pockets in horizontal main fuse; **3.** fuel filler cap; **4.** lifting lug; **5.** fuel tank;
6. Wire-bound compressed air spheres for pneumatic control motors; **7.**
Ram tube; **8.** Jet motor flanked by mixing venturis; **9.** Combustion chambers;
10. 400-ft. aerial for ranging transmitter; **11.** pneumatic motors to operate
controls; **12.** Battery, fuel and guidance controls; **13.** Wooden ribs (some
were metal) on tubular metal spar; **14.** Cable cutter (optional, one of two
forms); **15.** War-head; **16.** Air log to determine length of flight.

A cross-section of a V-1 Flying Bomb, showing mechanisms. *(Yorkshire Ridings Magazine)*

Luftwaffe were those in north-west Germany: eleven of them between Handorf (on about the same latitude as Felixstowe) and as far north as Leck near the Danish border, due east from Middlesbrough.

Although the distances were too great for a conventionally fired V-1 to do any damage to the Manchester area, the Christmas Eve 1944 attacks used another method. Around fifty Heinkel 111s were equipped with a V-1 attached beneath the starboard wing. Between 5 and 6 a.m. the missiles were launched at the north-west of England from over the North Sea. Manchester was the rough target area, possibly because if the missile overshot it would hit the Liverpool conurbation, and if it fell short, the West Riding industrial centres would be under threat.

East coast fishermen working in the pre-dawn darkness of the North Sea witnessed several V-1s being fired. The unstable and low-flying Heinkel would be brilliantly illuminated for several moments before the 'sling-shot' sent the flying bomb on its way, so in the early morning darkness and silence the bright light and the noise rendered the process very noticeable. It was potentially an easy target, but, caught unawares, the Humberside anti-aircraft guns and available fighters were unable to deal with the attack. At least one V-1 was seen plunging straight into the sea. (It was later revealed that nineteen of them had suffered this fate.) Of those that flew inland, a number failed to cross the Pennines. Constance Wright, at the time stationed at RAF Driffield 20 miles from the coast, recalls counting nine flaming missiles passing overhead. The first she thought was a plane on fire, a common initial mistake by those who saw the V-1 in flight. Ten – out of a total of around thirty that had made it past the coast – fell in Yorkshire, Humberside, and Lincolnshire. Two more hit the West Riding, but with little damage and no casualties: one in the hamlet of Grange Moor between Huddersfield and Wakefield, and another on open moorland on Midhope Moor about 10 miles to the south.

There is a general consensus about the sound the missile made: loud and unnerving, a thrumming, discordant growl, with frequent reference being made to a noisy motorbike. Tom Pollitt of Levenshulme recalled that 'it roared over with the sound of half a dozen Harleys' (www.levyboy.com). William Paul, of Clayton: 'It was like a drill but with a deeper tone.' Annie Taylor of the ill-fated Abbey Hills Road in Oldham remembered: 'It was horrible, like a heavy motorcycle going over the top.' (*Oldham Evening Chronicle*,

21 December 1994.) Jerry Hartley, who was living in Longsight at the time, recalls 'a gruff sound, like a high-powered motor bike'. Mr R. Heywood of Sharston: 'A dull pulsating roar ... that seemed to shake the bed.' (*Flying Bombs Over the* Pennines, p. 30.) The exact impression may have varied, depending on the height of the missile flight path and how close it was. Richard Young's description is perhaps the most vivid and comprehensive: 'The noise of its flight was hideous. It was coarser, louder, more blatant than the regular pulsation of ordinary aircraft ... A long flame of exhaust gave the whole ugly structure a fiendish kind of life.' (*The Flying Bomb*, p. 13.) And of course, when the engine noise suddenly ceased, it meant the bomb was on its way down to impact.

The locus of descent was unpredictable: sometimes the V-1 spiralled down, sometimes it made a right-angled turn, sometimes it continued along its flight path until gravity pulled it to earth in a steep dive. As ever, unpredictability added to the terror factor. In this lethal lottery, Greater Manchester had its winners and losers.

The worst hit was Abbey Hills Road in Oldham. The missile had passed over Lees Cemetery, about a kilometre to the east, and was heard on Balfour Street (off Lees Road) by Peter Dawson. He saw it low in the sky, recalling the grating roar and the long plume of flame. It was also witnessed by Elizabeth McNulty, who at the time was at an address in New Earth Street. She remembers that the dog had taken refuge under the table, which was apparently a familiar early warning of an air attack.

Wilfred Swan, an auxiliary fireman living on Orme Street, heard the air-raid siren, and then the detonation, audible for many miles around, at 5.50 a.m. Eighteen terraced houses on Abbey Hills Road were destroyed, and a similar number had to be demolished later. Over 1,000 houses within a three-quarter-mile radius were damaged. Wilfred arrived on the scene with the rescue squads, and recalls that there was a film of black dust and soot covering the streets and buildings.

Annie Taylor and her husband at No. 130 had the roof cave in on them, but were protected by the solid oak bed-head. At No. 151 the Kirklands and their holiday guests had mixed fortunes. Doreen Kirkland was located beneath collapsed beams by John Crowther, a 19-year-old ARP worker. John said that he thought he had heard a whimper from down below, and was lowered upside down into the wreckage to find its source. He wiped dirt from Doreen's mouth so she could breathe properly until the rescue could be carried out. Seventeen-year-old Kenneth Kirkland, still in his pyjamas, was digging through the rubble with his bare hands in an attempt to reach his younger brother David, aged 15. Eventually a policeman persuaded him to stop, and sent him away for a cup of tea from a neighbour. It was only later that it was discovered that David had been killed in the initial blast. He was one of four deaths at the address.

A number of macabre details emerged from reports of the Oldham carnage. Dismembered limbs had been flung by the blast into neighbouring houses. No trace was ever found of 62-year-old Hannah Holmes, a retired cotton worker who lived at No. 145. It would be the following May before she was formally named as a victim. Bodies had to be carried on makeshift stretchers to the temporary mortuary at Hope Congregational church a quarter of a mile away. There were thirty-two fatalities, and fifty-three people were seriously injured. It was by far the worst of the V-1 attacks on the north-west.

The missile had fulfilled another purpose, in that it was a bearer of propaganda leaflets, a bundle of which had been dropped into Lees Cemetery just before the engine cut out. They appeared to be letters from British POWs in Germany, with Christmas greetings and news of how well they were being treated in the camps, although the authenticity of the contents was questioned. Their aim was almost certainly to encourage replies, so that the German High Command would have some idea of where the bombs had landed. The bundles were confiscated by the police, and their ultimate release to the addressees was made on the strict condition that the contents were not made public.

The V-1 whose final destination was Worsley was heard flying over central Manchester. On Bank Street, Clayton, William Paul, who was celebrating his seventh birthday that day, was in an air-raid shelter when he heard the 'juddering' noise. The people in the shelter had been singing 'Daisy, Daisy', and then there was a 'sudden, frightened silence'. Olive Turnbull in Gorton, who worked for the munitions firm Vaughan Crane & Co. in Openshaw, heard the same 'unnerving sound'. Some children in Booth Hall Hospital in Blackley, evacuees from London, recognised the sound of the missile, and urged everyone, nurses included, to dive under the bed!

This V-1 continued on its westward path over Cheetham, Kersal Dale and Broughton until, above the junction of Worsley Road and the East Lancs. Road, the engine noise suddenly stopped, as witnessed by Robert Cliff and his family. They saw the flash of the explosion, and a couple of seconds later, heard the bang. The missile had fallen on Woodstock Drive, Worsley, a mile to the west. Four houses were destroyed, and there was minor damage in the neighbouring roads and woodland. There was one fatality: a 6 year old who was sleeping downstairs as he was convalescing from measles.

One missile, which made it over the Pennines but failed to cross the Greater Manchester conurbation, landed on Westwood Farm, off Mottram Road, a couple of miles to the east of Hyde town centre. It was a direct hit which killed two of the five occupants and many farm animals. This was the last missile to fall, at just before 6.30 a.m. The New Inn opposite the farm had its windows blown out. It is a sad footnote to this episode that whilst the farmer, Edwin Foulkes, was in hospital recuperating, the farm buildings were looted.

Closer to the intended target area, in Adswood, Stockport, another V-1 caused some damage, with one death and four serious injuries. ARP Warden C.E. Richardson was in the vicinity, and recalls: 'We saw the flash, but it was a very dark morning and we didn't know what

A V1 flying bomb on display at the Danish Museum of Military History. (*Nationalmuseet Copenhagen*)

road had been hit.' (*The Stockport Advertiser*, 29 December 1944.) This was at 5.30 a.m., the same time as the Worsley explosion. The impact area was on Garners Lane, with a bungalow, comprising Nos 87 and 89, receiving the worst of the blast. Every window was broken in the nearby Davenport Golf Course clubhouse (roughly where Bracadale Drive is now, near the fish ponds). The Methodist church and local school suffered broken and cracked panes.

The only flying bomb to land within the City of Manchester had travelled westwards over Stockport and Gatley, and began its descent over Sharston. This was the one with the 'dull, pulsating roar' described by Mr R. Heywood. Happily for the residents of Sharston – a heavily built-up area in Wythenshawe – the missile made a sharp 90° turn to the right, crossing the River Mersey and exploding harmlessly in a field of Brussels sprouts. The crater was a couple of hundred yards south of Underbank Farm, where the Old Bedians rugby clubhouse is now. There were no casualties or injuries, but windows as far away as Altrincham Road in Northenden and Fog Lane in Burnage were reported broken.

Models of a V-1 and a V-2 (the heavier, self-contained rocket bomb, which thankfully was never used against the north-west) went on display at the *Daily Express* exhibition in Lewis's on Market Street in January 1945. Even the reduced-size V-2 rocket on its concrete launch platform was a 'fearsome looking dummy', according to the *Guardian* report.

Press censorship meant that news of the Christmas Eve bombings scarcely made it to the newspapers, except in very vague and generalised terms. Even the résumé in the *Guardian* the following April omitted to mention precise locations:

FLYING BOMBS
Lancashire Towns that
Were Hit

One morning last December a flying bomb dropped in Oldham, demolishing some houses and damaging others. A number of people were killed and a large number were treated at the local infirmary for injuries. A large bundle of letters purporting to be from prisoners of war were found in a cemetery, where they had apparently fallen from the bomb. Addresses and regimental numbers were given.

People were killed and others injured on the same morning when a row of cottages at Tottington, near Bury, were destroyed. The old parish church which stands across the road from the cottages had all its windows blown out and its roof interior badly damaged. The school attached to the church was damaged beyond repair. Letters supposed to have been written by British war prisoners in Germany were dropped with this bomb. Services went on as usual in the damaged church. Two of the killed had arrived to spend a Christmas holiday with a relative only a few hours earlier.

One flying bomb fell in a field a short distance from the southern boundary of Manchester at Didsbury but did no damage.

(Manchester Guardian, 27 April 1945)

It had been the Nazis' final throw on the British mainland. Within eleven days of this *Guardian* report Hitler was dead, German forces had surrendered, and VE-Day was being celebrated.

NINE

'A FINER CITY WILL ARISE': PHOENIX MANCHESTER

• THE POET AND THE PAINTER •
• A CITY SPEAKS •
• RESTORATION, REHOUSING AND REBUILDING • THE FIRE WINDOW •

I have seen ghosts in daylight,
Heard their sighs,
Who walk on charred and
battered wreckage
Of their homes.
Seen iron girders, warped and twisted
like the souls of those
Who made them walk.
A roofless church, all open to the sky,
The empty pews inviting worship still,
From passers-by.
A scarlet dancing shoe – sad flotsam,
All that's left to mark
The spot where once a theatre's
magic glow
Lit up the dark …

Extract from a poem by
Marjorie Pullen
(*Manchester City News*,
15 March 1941)

In 1941, a couple of months after Marjorie Pullen had written her poem, Stockport artist James Chettle exhibited three paintings depicting the Manchester Blitz: *War Memorial*, *Bloody But Unbowed*, and *All Clear – Raiders Passed*. His *War Memorial* – the title has a deliberate irony – shows the remains of part of the warehouse district, looking along Portland Street. The foreground depicts a pair of gaunt, blasted towers, the only objects left standing over a sea of rubble and under a cloudscape of a haunting shade somewhere between grubby peach and ash-grey. In the background some buildings appear untouched, but it's the ruined turrets that dominate in a scene drained of primary colours and devoid of a focal point.

The scenes depicted in poem and painting are bleak, but the fact that decent art and literature were forged so soon from the fires of the Blitz is a stirringly positive sign. It suggests that the nightmares have been faced and transmuted; already the future, the time of healing and rebuilding, can be addressed.

Another work deserves our attention: *A City Speaks* was a major documentary film about post-war Manchester and its aspirations. It was directed by Paul Rotha and released in July 1947 after over two years of preparation. It contains the following quotation:

> *Oh God, grant us a vision of our city, fair as she might be:*
> *A city of justice, where none shall prey on others,*
> *A city of plenty, where vice and poverty shall cease to fester,*
> *A city of brotherhood …*
> *A city of peace …*

This is an extract from *Prayer for the City* by Walter Rauschenbusch (1910).

A City Speaks opens with these words as a voice-over as the aerial camera sweeps high above a huge metropolis of housing estates, parks and factories. It perhaps consciously references the opening sequence of Hitler's propaganda film *The Triumph of the Will*, except that here it is the city that takes centre stage, and not a glorified individual descending from the clouds in his aeroplane. The first individual seen in the Rotha film is an anonymous lad in short trousers who pauses in the Town Hall entrance to look at the statues of nineteenth-century Salford and Mancunian physics and chemistry giants Joule and Dalton. Thus the past and the future are neatly suggested in a moment of the present: the life of the city is shown as a continuum, unbroken by the recent havoc.

There were those who were wary of the possible airbrushing of reality in the film:

> What finer achievement for the civic film than it should show to Mancunians not only a proud past, and a great future, but those festering sores which still remain in our present-day society to shadow that future, and give citizens a most salutary 'surprise' and a determination to make a clean sweep of them quickly?
>
> (*City News* Editorial, 5 January 1945)

Bombsite and slum clearance, and building of new houses – some temporary, others more permanent – were of high priority in council planning, which had begun in theory as early as 1941. It would take many years before the scheme was completed, as for some time manpower and materials were in short supply. Aluminium-based 'prefabs' were in use soon after the end of the war, in the following locations:

Sheepfoot Lane	280
Heaton Park Main Drive	280
Wythenshawe Park (Moor Road/Altrincham Road)	300
Hough End Fields (Mauldeth Road West/Princess Road)	380
Lightbowne Road/Broadhurst Park	75
Charlestown Road/Boggart Hole Clough	150
Total	1,465

It took twelve workmen one working day to erect one of these houses. Interior fittings would be completed within the next two days. Originally intended as a temporary accommodation for the bombed-out, they were to last much longer: the writer can remember from the early 1960s the prefabs on Hough End playing fields and along the south-eastern side of Moor Road in Wythenshawe.

In January 1946 the council announced its housing targets: 12,800 new permanent homes by 1948, and 25,000 by 1951. Five hundred 'high priority cases' – such as ex-servicemen and their families – had already been provided for.

The rehousing process provoked some debate. For example, the design of some of the proposed houses was criticised by the Women's Advisory Sub-Committee on Housing, which made the following observation: 'Too small sinks and unnecessary dust-traps, hallmarks of houses in which women have had no say.' (*City News* Correspondence, 23 March 1945.)

The plan to import 30,000 temporary wooden houses from the USA (one of the last 'lease-lend' actions) had to be reconsidered. Of these 1,200 were destined for Manchester, until it was pointed out that they would not be a wise choice for the damp climate of north-west England. As a prospective tenant put it: 'I don't want my wife and youngsters to spend more than a couple of winters in a wooden house.' (*City News* Correspondence, 16 March 1945.)

There was further controversy when it was revealed that in order to build permanent brick and concrete homes for an estimated 1,200–1,500 families off Hall Lane in Wythenshawe, the nearby Baguley Hall Farm would have to be vacated. Protests came to nothing, and work began on what was to become the housing estate between Hall Lane and the present M56 motorway. German POWs began clearing the ground and laying roads and sewers. Nowadays the only remaining link with the past is the medieval Baguley Hall, a Grade I listed building.

The reconstruction of the city centre was slow but sure. The demolition of the damaged fabric of the Cotton Exchange was begun in 1947. Three years and £600,000 later, Boots the Chemist reopened on the ground floor, and there were seven storeys of offices that would be completely in use by the end of 1950. The building is now home to the Royal Exchange Theatre.

The rebuilding of the Free Trade Hall started in September 1949, and would be ready in time for the Festival of Britain in May 1951. The cost was nearly £400,000, which included a substantial contribution from the War Damage Commission. Soon to be once more the permanent home of the Hallé Orchestra, the Hall has also been the venue of many shows, events and concerts. Louis Armstrong, Andres Segovia, Yehudi Menuhin and Sir Adrian Boult are amongst the celebrated musicians who have performed here. It was here that the famous 'Judas!' Bob Dylan incident took place in 1966, and here that the Sex Pistols unleashed their New Wave contribution in a 1976 concert.

The sites of the gutted warehouses on the block adjacent to Piccadilly, once they had completed their purpose of housing static water tanks, were turned into car parks by the 1950s. Nowadays the ultra-modern Piccadilly Plaza and Mercure Hotel overlook the new bus station and island tram stop, the big wheel and the fountains, and, of course, the Second World War memorial tree. Where buckled tramlines and debris once blocked the surrounding streets, the Metrolink now smoothly runs, connecting the city centre to the satellite towns and the airport.

The Bradford/Philips Park area in east Manchester with its power station on Stuart Street and gas, iron and chemical works, was a prime Luftwaffe target in 1940–41. In place of the industrial behemoths and surrounding slums there now stand the Etihad Campus – Manchester City's home stadium since 2003 – and the National Cycling Centre. This complex was the hub of the 2002 Commonwealth Games. The central north–south road system which used to comprise Forge Lane, Mill Street and Grey Mare Lane has been rebuilt into a dual carriageway and renamed Alan Turing Way, in honour of the Mancunian who made a major contribution to the Bletchley Park code-breaking, a significant factor in the Allies' Second World War victory.

Westwards along the Irwell/Ship Canal in Salford, where the Docks were once ablaze, the Quays now boast select apartments, and the spectacular architecture and bustling activity of Media City UK and the BBC hub, the Lowry, and the Imperial War Museum North.

Perhaps the most striking modern-day contrast with the Blitz years is eminently visible over the Knott Mill and Great Bridgewater Street area at the southern end of Deansgate. Where once there were cratered streets, the smoking rubble of warehouses, and mangled railway lines there now soars the giant gleaming slab of the 2006 Beetham/Hilton Tower, at over 550ft the tallest building in England outside London.

We will end this story more or less where it began on 22 December 1940: in the cathedral. The building would not be fully restored until July 1957, with a thanksgiving service planned for the second week in September of that year. As the new dean, the Reverend H.A. Jones, put it: 'By then, I hope, we will be free at last from the sounds of axes and hammers and saws …' Total cost of restoration came to £200,000, half of which was contributed once more by the War Damage Commission, and half of which came from public donations to the appeal fund. This fund, of course, had been managed by former dean Dr Garfield Williams until his retirement in 1948.

The Military chapel was rebuilt according to the design of architect Mr T. Worthington, an ex-captain of the Manchester Regiment.

Repairs on the cathedral were not fully completed until 1958. *(Manchester Evening News)*

After military amalgamations it now bears the name of the Chapel of the Duke of Lancaster's Regiment. At its north-east corner the fire window replaced the old stained-glass window in 1963, and was dedicated in 1966. The artist was Margaret Traherne, who penned the following about her creation:

I wanted to give the feeling of battle and fire but also a religious quality. To allow people to form their own thoughts and make their own deductions whilst standing before it and watching the way the colours work. The dominant colour of the window is red. Red is the colour of alarm and of the human passions, which lead to death. Red is also the colour of fire with its ancient associations not only with war but with sacrifice and the glory of resurrection.

(Manchester Cathedral – Official Guide)

The fire window never fails to draw and hold the eye. Red, orange and yellow blades and slivers of flame jostle and overlap on their climb to the top of the arch, and if the sun is shining through the panes the effect is stunning. It suffered minor damage after the June 1996 bomb, but was soon restored.

Beneath the window, on the altar cloth, there is a design of a phoenix. The symbolism is obvious, but no less fitting and powerful for that: fulfilling the New Year 1941 prophecy of the Lord Mayor Alderman R.G. Edwards, a finer city has indeed arisen from the ashes of the Blitz. Pure pragmatists may argue with some justifica-

tion that there is still work to be done, but for romantics and those with a sense of the people's history one thing remains true: despite the destruction and upheavals of yesteryear the Spirit of Manchester continues undimmed into the twenty-first century.

(Author's collection)

APPENDICES

APPENDIX 1:   Manchester Emergency Committee's Log of Bombing
Incidents 22–24 December 1940 *(source: Emergency
Committee Records/Police Museum and Archives)*

APPENDIX 2:   Stretford Bombing Incidents 22–24 December 1940
(source: Trafford Archives and Luftwaffe Over
Manchester – *see bibliography)*

APPENDIX 3:   Salford Bombing Incidents September 1940 – June 1941
*(source: Salford Control Centre Air Raid Warning
Messages/Salford Local History Archives)*

APPENDIX 4:   Manchester Rest Centres During the Blitz
*(source: Emergency Committee Minutes/
Police Museum and Archives)*

APPENDIX 5:   Stretford Rest Centres During the Blitz
(source: Trafford Archives)

APPENDIX 6:   Luftwaffe Reconnaissance Maps: Salford Docks Area
(source: Trafford Archives)

APPENDIX 7:   Salford Rest Centres During the Blitz
(source: Manchester Evening News, *17 December 1940)*

APPENDIX 8:   Manchester and Salford Bombing Maps
*(source: Manchester Libraries Information and Archives,
Salford Local History Archives)*

APPENDIX 9:   Anti-aircraft Placements Around Manchester in the
Second World War
(source: AA Command – *see bibliography)*

APPENDIX 1

MANCHESTER EMERGENCY COMMITTEE'S LOG OF BOMBING INCIDENTS 22–24 DECEMBER 1940

These reports were logged in the order they were received, and the final list compiled at Bootle Street Police Station on 29 December 1940. They are mostly concerned with 'A' Division incidents, or the city centre. 'B' Division was Miles Platting/Crumpsall area. 'C' Bradford and Gorton, 'D' Rusholme and Longsight.

H.E. =	High Explosive
I.B. =	Incendiary Bomb
D.H. =	Dwelling House
C-on-M =	Chorlton-on-Medlock
AFS =	Auxiliary Fire Service
ARP =	Air Raid Precautions
CWS =	Co-operative Wholesale Society
C.P.A. =	Calico Printers' Association
B.D.A. =	Bradford Dyers' Association
F.A. =	First Aid

SUMMARY OF INCIDENTS OCCURRING ON THE 'A' DIVISION ON THE NIGHT OF 22 & 23 DECEMBER 1940

NUMBERS THAT ARE GROUPED TOGETHER REFER TO THE SAME INCIDENT OR CONFLAGRATION

1. ALBERT SQUARE & PRINCESS ST
   Incendiary bomb. Fire caused to 29 Princess St 7.10 p.m.
   22nd. Incident closed and again opened at 6.00 p.m.
   23rd. Incident finally closed at 7.51 a.m. 27th inst.

2. BRIDGEWATER ST & CHEPSTOW ST
   I.B. extinguished and incident closed. 7.10 p.m. 22nd.

3. DEVONSHIRE ST & PUMP ST, HULME
   – do –

4. CATHEDRAL YARD; 5. CATHEDRAL ST; 7. CORN EXCHANGE; 13. FENNEL STREET
   EXCHANGE HOTEL; 85. ROYAL EXCHANGE; 105. DEANSGATE – VICTORIA ST;
   164. LONG MILLGATE; 166. CROSS ST – CATHEDRAL WALKS; CATHEDRAL HOUSE
   Shower of incendiary bombs were dropped at 7.10 p.m.
   22nd which caused numerous fires. H.E. bombs were
   dropped at approx. 10.50 p.m. and later a mine. Serious
   damage was caused by fire in this vicinity, including
   St Mary's Gate and Deansgate. Incident not finally closed.

6. ODEON CINEMA
   Incendiary bomb. Extinguished and
   incident closed 1.38 a.m. 23rd.

8. MARLBORO' ST; 9 WHITWORTH ST WEST
   Incendiary bomb 7.15 p.m. 22nd.
   Incident closed 12.8 a.m. 23rd.

10. GAYTHORN GASWORKS
    Incendiary bomb 7.15 p.m. 22nd.
    Extinguished and incident closed.

11. STRETFORD RD & WILMOTT ST, HULME
    Incendiary bomb 7.30 p.m. 22nd. Damage to shop.
    Fire extinguished and incident closed. No persons injured.

12. WHITWORTH ST & OXFORD ST
Incendiary bomb 7.20 p.m. 22nd. Incident closed at once.

14. GREEK ST & GROSVENOR ST, C-ON-M
Incendiary bomb 10.00 p.m. 22nd. Walls of warehouse
damaged. No persons injured. Incident closed 7.59 a.m. 23rd.

15. GLOUCESTER ST & WHITWORTH ST WEST
Incendiary bomb on roof of Hotspur Press.
Damage to roof. Fire extinguished and incident closed.

16. C.P.A. OXFORD ST
Incendiary bomb in Main Gate 7.15.
Fire extinguished and incident closed at 12.08 a.m. 23rd.

17. BRAZENNOSE ST & ALBERT SQUARE
Incendiary bomb approx. 7.30 p.m. Fires caused in Brazennose
Chambers and 9 Albert Square. Extinguished and incident closed.

18. LLOYD ST & ALBERT SQUARE
Incendiary bomb 7.30 p.m. 22nd.
Extinguished and incident closed.

19. CEDAR ST, RUSSELL ST, TOWSON ST, HULME
Incendiary bomb. 7.30 p.m. 22nd. Fire in roof of 16 Towson
St also at 30 Cedar St Both extinguished and incidents closed
at 12.20 a.m. 23rd. Slight damage to cottage property.

20. OLYMPIA GARAGE; 77. KNOTT MILL; 133. – ; 134. –
Incendiary bomb 7.35 p.m. 22nd. Followed by H.E. at
9.29 p.m. and again 1.50 a.m. 23rd. Extensive damage to
surrounding property in Owen St, Riga St and Knott Mill-
Deansgate. Gas main fractured. Nine persons rendered
homeless and sent to Zion Inst; two slight casualties.

21. CAMBRIDGE ST & GEORGE ST (DUNLOPS)
29. Incendiary bomb a6 [*sic*] 7.15 p.m. 22nd. Followed by
H.E. Damage to roof of premises. Three slight casualties
due to fumes from chemical extinguishers used by
employees of Dunlops. Incident later closed.

22. PREMISES AT JUNCTION OF ATHERTON ST & ST JOHN'S PLACE
Incendiary bomb at 7.39 p.m. 22nd.
Warden broke in and extinguished fire.
Damage to upper floor and roof. Incident closed.

23. TIMBER YARD. CITY RD & MEDLOCK ST
Incendiary bomb at 7.30 p.m. 22nd. Slight fire
extinguished and incident closed at 12.08 a.m. 23rd.

24. BOOTH ST & BROWN ST, CITY
Incendiary bomb at 7.50 p.m. 22nd.
Extinguished. No fire to property.

25. IMPERIAL BLDGS, OXFORD RD
Incendiary bomb at 7.30 p.m. 22nd.
Extinguished. No fire to property.

26. CRAWSHAW ST & COOKE ST, C-ON-M
Incendiary bomb at 7.10 p.m. 22nd. Fire on top
floor of 4 Cooke St (warehouse). Extinguished
by fire brigade and incident later closed.

27. GILLOW ST, OFF BYROM ST, CITY
Incendiary bomb at 7.32 p.m. 22nd. Extinguished
by wardens. Slight damage to cottage property.

28. QUEEN ST, CITY
This incident relates to incident No. 17.

29. SEE NO. 21

30. KING ST, SHIP CANAL HOUSE & 78 KING ST
Incendiary bomb at 7.45 p.m. 22nd. Slight damage to 78
King St. Fire extinguished and incident closed at 1.36 a.m. 23rd.

31. GARAGE, LOWER MOSLEY ST – GREAT BRIDGEWATER ST
Incendiary bomb at 7.10 p.m. 22nd.
Slight fire extinguished and incident closed.

32. WINDMILL ST & WATSON ST, CITY; 55. FREE TRADE HALL; 36 PETER ST
Incendiary bomb at 8.12 p.m. 22nd. Resulted
in major incident in which Free Trade Hall was
destroyed, also railway warehouse in Watson St and
Windmill St. Incident still open. [29/12/40]

33. CHRISTIAN SCIENCE CHURCH, PETER ST
Incendiary bomb 7.20 p.m. 22nd. Slight fire in
rafters. Extinguished and incident closed.

34. PORTLAND ST; SACKVILLE ST; SILVER ST
Incendiary bombs 7.50 p.m. 22nd. Major incident.
Several warehouses gutted. Incident still open
[29/12/40]. Under military control.

35. FAWCETT ST & CLARENDON ST, HULME
Incendiary bomb at 7.30 p.m. 22nd. Extinguished
by wardens. No damage. Incident closed.

36. ST GEORGE'S PARK, MIDGELEY'S SOAP WORKS, CITY RD, HULME
(APPROX. 7.30 P.M.). [ALSO SEE INCIDENTS 177 &179]
Shower of approx. 150 incendiary bombs. All extinguished
on park at once. Fire started on roof of Messrs Midgeley's
Soap Works, 325 City Road. Public shelter under premises
was evacuated. One slight casualty. Incident closed.

37. BRIDGEWATER ST & DEANSGATE
Incendiary bomb at 7.35 p.m. 22nd.
Extinguished and incident closed.

38. TONMAN ST & DEANSGATE
Incendiary bomb at 7.45 p.m. 22nd. Fire on roof of
London Metal warehouses, Tonman St. Extinguished
by fire brigade and incident closed, 9.05 p.m. 22nd.

39. MULBERRY ST ALBERT SQ. END
Incendiary bomb approx. 7.45 p.m. 22nd.
Extinguished and incident closed.

40. PRESCOTT ST & CITY RD, HULME
Incendiary bomb at 7.35 p.m. 22nd. Slight damage to cottage
property. Fire extinguished and incident closed 12.30 a.m. 23rd.

41. DRYBURGH PLACE, STRETFORD RD, HULME
Incendiary bomb at 7.40 p.m. 22nd. Warehouse
property damaged by fire. Extinguished by fire
brigade and incident closed at 12.08 a.m. 23rd.

42. BRAZENNOSE ST & DEANSGATE
Incendiary bomb at 7.50 p.m. 22nd.
Extinguished and incident closed.

43. ATKINSON ST & DEANSGATE
Incendiary bomb at 7.50 p.m. 22nd. Slight damage
to property. Fire extinguished and incident closed.

44. PICKERING ST, CHESTER ROAD
Incendiary bomb approx. 7.35 p.m. 22nd.
Extinguished and incident closed.

45. JACKSON'S ROW [AND 52. CITY]
Shower of incendiary bombs at approx. 7.45 p.m.
started several fires in this vicinity. Beatty's warehouse
was gutted. Fire extinguished and incident closed.

46. St Ann's Square, St Ann Street

Shower of incendiary bombs at approx. 8.10 p.m. started several fires in the district. Messrs. Marshall & Snelgroves, Olivant & Botsford, Equitable Buildings etc., are extensively damaged by fire. Incident still in charge of fire brigade.

47. Charles St & Leigh St

Incendiary bomb at 7.20 p.m. 22nd. Damage by fire to warehouse property, 31 Charles St. Extinguished by fire brigade and incident closed.

48. Mosley St & Piccadilly. Parker St [see No. 132]

Shower of incendiary bombs at approx. 8.25 p.m. 22nd. Fires were started at 7-9-11-13 Mosley St, rapidly spreading to York St, back George St, George St, and along Parker St to Portland St. Incident still open and in charge of the Military Authorities. Blasting is taking place in the gutted buildings.

49. Gray St & Oxford Rd

Incendiary bomb at 8.55 p.m. 22nd. Extinguished by wardens. Incident closed. No damage.

50. Commercial St, Knott Mill

Incendiary bomb at 8.05 p.m. 22nd. Fire on roof of Carriers W'House. Extinguished by fire brigade. Incident closed. PC injured by blast.

51. Bale St & Lower Mosley St

Incendiary bombs at 7.55 p.m. 22nd. Fire on roof of B.D.A. Spread rapidly to nearby buildings. Dingley's, Lewis's Jewellers, damaged by fire. Two AFS workers injured. Incident reopened 26th. Now closed.

52. City [see No. 45]

53. Tib St & Whittle St

Incendiary bomb at 8.25 p.m. 22nd. Extinguished and incident closed. Shop property damaged.

54. ST GEORGE'S PARK, HULME
Three H.E. bombs at 8.35 p.m. 22nd.
One hit empty sunken shelter, one in paddling pool
and one on open park ground. No casualties.

56. POTATO WHARF, LIVERPOOL RD
Incendiary bomb at 8.19 p.m. 22nd. Damage
by fire to Abbott's Warehouse. Extinguished
by fire brigade and incident closed.

57. CASTLEFIELD & DEANSGATE
H.E. bomb at 8.00 p.m. 22nd. Two Manchester
Ship Canal warehouses and cottage property
damaged. No fire. Incident closed.

58. C.W.S. BALLOON ST
Incendiary bomb at 8.20 p.m. 22nd. Only slight damage to
building. Fire extinguished by CWS firemen. Incident closed.

59. ST MATTHEW'S CHURCH, LIVERPOOL ROAD
Incendiary bomb on church roof at 8.20 p.m. 22nd.
Slight damage. Extinguished by fire brigade. Incident closed.

60. SPEAR ST & HOULDSWORTH ST
Incendiary bomb on warehouse property at 8.30 p.m. 22nd.
Extinguished by fire brigade and incident closed at 9.08 p.m.

61. GREEK ST & 63. BEDFORD ST, C-ON-M
Incendiary bombs at 9.30 p.m. 22nd. Extinguished and
incidents closed. Damage to warehouse property.

64. ST AUGUSTINE'S, 158. YORK ST, C-ON-M
Incendiary bombs on the district at 8.55 p.m. 22nd. Fires were
extinguished and incident closed. On early morning of 23rd
a parachute mine struck the vicinity of the same incident,
causing extensive damage to surrounding property, rendered
homeless 341 persons. One male killed. Two female
persons killed. One male injured. Incident now closed.

65. SMITHFIELD MARKET
[MAJOR INCIDENT – SEE NOS 74, 92, 100, 106, 171]
Shower of incendiary bombs in the vicinity of the Market
at 8.20 p.m. 22nd. Damage was caused to the roof and
various stalls and offices in the Wholesale and Retail Fish
and Produce Markets. Several premises in Swan St were
extensively damaged by fire. Fires were extinguished by
the fire brigade, and the incidents were later closed.

66. SACKVILLE ST & MOUNT ST, C-ON-M
Incendiary bombs at 9.10 p.m. 22nd. Warehouse property
damaged by fire. Ivy Mills, Sackville St, extensively damaged.
Gutted. Fires extinguished by fire brigade and incident closed.

67. MOUNT ST, NEAR [CENTRAL] LIBRARY
Incendiary bomb at 7.50 p.m. 22nd. Slight damage to shop
property. Extinguished by police and incident closed 8.00 p.m.

68. 36 GEORGE ST, CITY
Incendiary bomb at 7.10 p.m. 22nd.
No fire. Incident closed. 7.20 p.m.

69. LITTLE PETER ST, CITY ROAD
Incendiary bomb at 7.00 p.m. 22nd.
Extinguished by warden. Incident closed 7.15 p.m.

70. 78 KING ST, CITY OTTOMAN BANK, CROSS ST
Incendiary bombs on roofs of premises at
8.45 p.m. 22nd. Damage by fire to top floors of
office premises. Fire extinguished by fire brigade
and incident closed at 1.05 p.m. 23rd.

71. WILMOTT ST & CLARENDON ST, HULME
Incendiary bombs at 9.15 p.m. 22nd. Damage by fire
to cottage and warehouse property. Fire extinguished
by fire brigade and incident closed. 11.37 p.m.

72. WATER ST & 81 HARDMAN ST, FAULKNER'S
Incendiary bomb at 9.15 p.m. 22nd. Faulkner's
warehouse gutted by fire. Incident closed.

73. SIDNEY ST, C-ON-M POST OFFICE
Incendiary bomb at 8.55 p.m. 22nd. Post office damaged
by fire. Fire extinguished by fire brigade and incident closed.

74. NORTH ST & MILLER ST, CITY, 29 MILLER ST
[SEE NOS 65, 92, 100, 106, 171]
Incendiary bombs at 9.00 p.m. 22nd.
Shop and warehouse extensively damaged by fire.
Fire extinguished and incident closed.

75. KING ST WEST & ALBERT ST
Shower of Incendiary bombs in this area at 9.28 p.m.
22nd. Whole of block bounded by Motor St, Albert
St, King St West were [sic] practically gutted by fires.
One H.E. dropped at the junction of Albert St and King
St West. No persons injured. Incident now closed.

76. TRADES SUPPLY, CITY RD & GT JACKSON ST
H.E. bomb struck rear of Trades Supply causing collapse
of building. Damage was caused to windows and doors of
Jackson St Police Station. One male casualty. No persons
complained of injury in the public shelter under premises.

78. WHEATSHEAF HOTEL, DEANSGATE
Incendiary bomb on roof at 7.30 p.m. Damage to slates and by
fire. Extinguished by AFS and incident closed at 9.42 p.m. 22nd.

79. DEANSGATE & CHESTER RD
Reported H.E. bomb at 9.30 p.m. 22nd. No further particulars.

80. SWAN ST, BETWEEN OAK ST & TIB ST
Incendiary bomb approx. 9.00 p.m. 22nd.
Serious damage caused to 19 – 19a – 23 & 21 Swan St,
by fire. Incident now closed. 12.10 p.m. 23rd.

81. LEES ST & GT ANCOATS ST
Incendiary bomb at 9.25 p.m. 22nd. Damage caused by
fire to Viney's Garage. Fire extinguished. Incident closed.

82. FAULKNER'S YARD, WATER ST
Manchester Ship Canal Warehouse was also damage
[*sic*] by fire. One nearby Dwelling House was also
damaged by fire. Three AFS men were injured by
bursting petrol tank, treated at First-Aid Post.

83. TAYLOR ST, OFF OXFORD RD
Incendiary bomb at 8.55 p.m. 22nd.
Extinguished and incident closed at once.

84. BRIDGE ST, CARTER ILES
Shower of incendiary bombs approx. 8.05 p.m. 22nd.
Premises Bridge St, between Deansgate and
Motor St caught fire. Most of fire spreading from
lower end of Bridge St. Incident now closed.

86. TRENTHAM ST & CHESTER RD
H.E. bomb on Cornbrook Brewery 9.45 p.m. Public shelter
below damaged and large number of dwelling houses. Some
persons in the shelter and later reported that ten bodies had
been recovered. Damage to gas and water mains. Remainder
of people were removed to sunken shelters at St George's
Park. Unexploded bomb reported in Chester Rd near to
King St. All people in vicinity were evacuated and attention
was given by Bomb Disposal Unit. Road now open.

87. CITY RD, BETWEEN BRADBURY ST AND ERSKINE ST
H.E. bomb on premises. Public shelter underneath.
People removed. No casualties.
Danger removed and incident closed.

88. 77 PRINCESS ST, 72 MOSLEY ST
Incendiary bomb approx. 7.45 p.m. 22nd. Fire on top
floor of 77 Princess St. Fire brigade attended and left,
but fire restarted and the office premises were gutted.

89. Universal Furs, Bridge St
Incendiary bomb approx. 9.00 p.m. 22nd. Fire in
premises. Extinguished by wardens and incident closed.

90. Milton St & Lower Moss Lane
Incendiary bomb at 9.25 p.m. 22nd.
Extinguished at once and incident closed.

91. Gibson's Erskine St, Hulme
Incendiary bomb on roof. Slight fire.
Extinguished and incident closed.

92. Joint with incident No. 74
[Also see Incidents 65, 100, 106, 171] [East of Victoria
Station – Shudehill and Smithfield Market area]
Other incendiary bombs in the vicinity caused extensive
damage to warehouse property. Incident still open.

93. Cooke St & Brook St, C-on-M
Incendiary bombs at 10.00 p.m. 22nd. Extinguished
by wardens and incidents closed. Slight damage
was caused to warehouse property.

95. St John's St & Deansgate
Incendiary bomb on roof of premises 8.45 p.m. 22nd. Slight
damage. Extinguished by AFS and incident closed. 1.5 a.m. 23rd.

96. Buxton St & London Rd
H.E. bomb at 10.05 p.m. 22nd. Taken over by 'C' Division.

97. Berwick St & Brook St
Incendiary bomb approx. 10.00 p.m. 22nd. Fire quickly
extinguished. No further report. Slight damage to shop property.

98. Havelock Mills, 138. 76 Great Bridgewater St
Incendiary bomb at 9.15 p.m. 22nd. Fire, top floor of warehouse
seriously damaged. Fire extinguished 1.55 a.m. Incident closed.

99. MAYFIELD STATION [SEE NO. 107]
H.E. bomb at 10.00 p.m. 22nd. Taken over by 'C' Division.

100. JOINT WITH INCIDENT 74 & 92
Incendiary bomb at 8.35 p.m. 22nd. Damage to 12 Mayes St.

102. DEANSGATE VIADUCT, CHURCH
Incendiary bomb at 9.05 p.m. 22nd. Fire damage 3rd Church
of Christ Scientist [*sic*]. Incident closed at 11.45 p.m.

103. 15 CROSS ST
Incendiary bomb at 10.25 p.m. 22nd. Slight
fire. Incident closed 11.30 p.m.

104. WILSON ST, OFF BURY ST, LONDON RD
H.E. bomb at 10.00 p.m. Taken over by 'C' Division.

105. CROSS ST & CHAPEL WALKS
Incendiary bomb at 10.20 p.m. 22nd.
Incident closed 9.40 p.m. 23rd. No further report of damage.

106. JOINT WITH INCIDENT NO. 65. SMITHFIELD MKT
Hare & Hounds Hotel, Shudehill. Incendiary bomb
at 9.30 p.m. 22nd. 48 Shudehill gutted by fire.
No. 50 slightly damaged. Incident closed at 6.05 a.m. 23rd.

107. MAYFIELD STATION [SEE NO. 99]
Incendiary bomb at 10.50 p.m. 22nd.
Taken over by 'C' Division.

108. SHEFFIELD ST & TRAVIS ST
H.E. bomb at 10.00 p.m. Crater in roadway. Incident still open.

109. 7 ST JAMES SQ. [SEE NO. 128]
Incendiary bomb at 11.10 p.m. 22nd. Damage to office property.
Incident finally closed at 7.41 p.m. 25th.

110. CAMBRIDGE ST & CHESTER ST, HULME
Incendiary bomb at 10.50 p.m. 22nd. Slight damage to
Messrs Dunlop's. Incident closed at 1.15 a.m. 23rd.

111. JORDON [*SIC*] ST & KNOTT MILL
Incendiary bomb at 10.35 p.m. 22nd. No report of
fire damage. Incident closed at 1.15 a.m. 23rd.

112. BACK GREEK ST, C-ON-M
Incendiary bomb at 10.35 p.m. 22nd. Slight fire damage
to D.H. property. Incident closed at 11.27 p.m.

113. 19 CLARE ST, ST LUKE'S ST, C-ON-M
Incendiary bomb at 8.50 p.m. 22nd. Slight fire at
D.H. Extinguished by wardens. Incident closed by 11.30 p.m.

114. ELLESMERE ST, HULME
Incendiary bomb at 11.23 p.m. 22nd. Fire in warehouse
property. No report of damage. Incident closed at 4 p.m. 26th.

115. BLOSSOM ST, HULME
Incendiary bomb at 11.10 p.m. 22nd. Extinguished
by wardens. Incident immediately closed.

116. JOINT WITH INCIDENTS 32 & 55, 36 PETER ST, CITY
Incendiary bombs. This incident at 36 Peter St is now closed.

117. 94 DUKE ST, STRETFORD RD
Incendiary bomb at 9.45 p.m. 22nd. Damage to
roof. Fire extinguished by PC and incident closed.

118. 100 PORTLAND ST, LLOYDS WAREHOUSE
Incendiary bomb at 11.40 p.m. 22nd. Serious fire to warehouse
property. Also spread to Women's Labour Exchange which
is seriously damaged. Incident closed at 9 p.m. 24th.

119. 64 DEVONSHIRE ST, 86 DUKE ST, HULME
Incendiary bomb at 7.50 p.m. 22nd. Damage to cottage
property. Extinguished by PC. Incident closed at 1.05 a.m. 23rd.

120. 22 Bridge St, City
Joint with nos 74 & 85 [*sic*]. Damage by incendiary bombs.

121. 46/48 Ellesmere St, Hulme
Incendiary bomb at 11.30 p.m. 22nd. Through roof.
Damage by fire to top floor. Extinguished by
AFS Unit and incident closed 2.05 a.m. 23rd.

122. Veterinary stables, Grosvenor St, C-on-M
Incendiary bomb at 11.45 p.m. 22nd.
No damage. Incident closed immediately.

123. 97 Portland St, City
Incendiary bomb at 12.45 a.m. 23rd. Fire was soon
under control, but broke out again. The building was
gutted and incident was closed on afternoon of 23rd.

124. 11 Peter St, City
Incendiary bomb at 7.30 p.m. 22nd. Only slight damage.
Fire extinguished and incident closed immediately.

125. 64 Market St, 67/69 Market St
Some of shower of incendiary bombs 12.30 a.m. 23rd. Both
buildings are seriously damaged by fire. Incidents now closed.

126. Byrom St & Camp St
Incendiary bomb at 12.20 a.m. 23rd. Damage to
D.H. property. Fire out and Incident closed. No time given.

127. Whitworth St West, 135. Albion St
H.E. bomb, reported UXB (parachute mine). Later found
that bomb had exploded, forming crater in road. Occurred
about 1.00 a.m. 23rd. Incident closed at 4.00 a.m. 23rd.

128. 6 St James Sq. [see no.109]
Incendiary bomb at 12.55 a.m. 23rd. Serious damage to
office property. Incident closed at 12.55 a.m. 23rd. [*sic*]

129. DUKE ST & CLARENDON ST
H.E. bomb at 1.20 a.m. 23rd. Damage to
surrounding D.H. property. Incident closed.

130. LEAF ST, DIXON ST, TOMLINSON ST, CLARENDON ST, NORTH ST
[NE OF HULME TOWN HALL]
Obviously same incident as above. Extensive damage
to D.H. property. Number of persons trapped under
wreckage. Fire broke out. Several dead removed to
mortuary and some injured to hospital. Suspected that
more persons are under debris. Incident still open.

131. HIGH ST & CHURCH ST, CITY
Incendiary bomb at 10.00 p.m. 22nd. Fire in shop property
extinguished by fire brigade and incident closed at 5.30 a.m. 23rd.

132. MARBLE ST & MOSLEY ST [SEE NO. 48]
Fire broke out at 24 Mosley St, this apparently arising
from fire at 9/15 Mosley St Message at 1.37 a.m. 23rd.

136. CLEANSING DEPT., WATER ST YARD
Reported UXB 2.00 a.m. Search made by Police.
No trace and incident closed. 4.00 a.m. 23rd.

137. CHESTER RD, BLANTYRE ST
H.E. bomb at 1.50 a.m. 23rd. Damage to surrounding
D.H. property. No casualties reported. Incident closed.

139. EXCHANGE STATION APPROACH
H.E. bomb at 1.50 a.m. 23rd. One stretcher case from
No. 5 Arch, Cathedral Arches. No other particulars.

140. ANGLE ST & CLARENDON ST, C-ON-M
Incendiary bomb at 2.40 a.m. 23rd. Fire in rafters of shop 60
Oxford Rd. Extinguished and incident closed at 4.00 a.m. 23rd.

141. DEVONSHIRE ST & 146. LOWER ORMOND ST
H.E. bomb in carriageway, 3.00 a.m. 23rd. Gas main
fractured. One casualty. Incident closed at 5.00 a.m. 27th.

143. Devonshire St & Cambridge St
H.E. bomb at 3.00 a.m. 23rd. Shop and D.H. property
damaged. Incident closed 5.00 a.m. 23rd.
[Last three incidents took place in the same small
area in C-on-M. See also Nos 145/6.]

144. Grape St, between Byrom St & Water St
Incendiary bombs at 2.10 a.m. 23rd. Fell onto loaded
railway lorries. Three lorries on fire. No damage to
other property. Incident closed at 4.00 a.m.

145. Grosvenor St & Brook St
Incendiary bomb at 3.05 a.m. 23rd. Fell on gutter of shop
62 Brook St. Extinguished and incident closed 9.30 a.m.

146. Devonshire St & 141. Lower Ormond St
Relating to same incident. Action Post
No.6 telephone put out of order.

147. Bridgewater Offices, Gt. Jackson St & Chester Rd
Incendiary bomb reported dropped at 3.40 a.m. 23rd.
Damage to building was apparently caused by blast from
H.E. bomb at Castle St & Deansgate. Incident closed 23rd.

148. Nuttall St, 151. Humphrey St, Wilmott St [Off Cambridge St,
400 yds south of Oxford Rd Railway Station]
H.E. dropped, possibly parachute mine at 4.10 a.m.
23rd. Many houses were demolished. Approx.
fifteen persons killed. Incident still open.

149. 141/145 Lower Moss Lane, Hulme
H.E. bomb at 4.0 a.m. 23rd. Three houses were
demolished and others damaged by blast. One dead,
one injured. Incident closed 6.45 a.m. 23rd.

150. York St & City Rd, Hulme
Incendiary bomb at 4.10 a.m. 23rd.
One person injured. Incident closed at 5.15 a.m. 23rd.

152. ARP POST, CATHEDRAL ST

H.E. at 4.55 a.m. 23rd. Struck side of building at
Corn Exchange and wrecked the warden's post at Cathedral St.
Two slight casualties, attended to by wardens. Incident closed.

153. CORPORATION ST & HOPWOOD AVE.

H.E. bomb at 4.55 p.m. 23rd. Fire at Burton's Stores,
Hopwood Ave. One casualty, but no further particulars.
Two UXB reported were found to be bombs which had been
on exhibition at a previous date. Incident now closed.

154. 7 THORNILEY BROW [BETWEEN DANTZIC ST & SHUDEHILL]

H.E. bomb at 4.55 p.m. 23rd. Fire extinguished. Damage
to other property, including Pifco. Ltd. Incident closed.

155. CANNON ST, 156. CORPORATION ST, MARKET PLACE.
KENYON'S VAULTS [OLD WELLINGTON INN]

H.E. bomb at 5.00 a.m. 23rd. Damage to surrounding
property. three casualties. Taken to F.A. Post. Fire threatening
other property. Gas main burning freely. Incident closed at
5.00 a.m. Reopened and again closed at 6.10 p.m. 24th.

157. AFS STATION, POTATO WHARF

H.E. at approx: 5.00 a.m. 23rd. Station suffered damage.
One AFS man injured. Sent to Roby St. Incident closed.

159. VICTORIA STATION

Incendiary bomb at 5.12 a.m. 23rd.
Reported four stretcher cases. No other information.

160 STAFFORD ST & BROOK ST, C-ON-M

H.E. bomb at 5.00 a.m. 23rd. Damage to works and
warehouse property. One female body taken from under
debris at 20 Stafford St. Incident closed at 1.46 p.m. 25th.

161. SPRING GARDENS, 76 MARKET ST

H.E. bomb at 5.00 a.m. 23rd. One male shock
casualty found in window of damaged shop. Taken
to Roby St. Incident closed 5.00 a.m.

162. 1ST AID POST, GARTSIDE ST
Incendiary bomb at 2.45 a.m. 23rd. Fire controlled
and extinguished. Incident closed at once.

163. 86 HARDMAN ST
Incendiary bomb at 2.45 a.m. 23rd. Fire controlled
and extinguished. Incident closed at once.

165. CITY RD & RIVER PLACE
H.E. bomb at 6.00 a.m. 23rd. Fell in corner of works yard.
Damage to wooden hoarding. No other apparent damage.
Incident closed 10.00 a.m. 23rd.

167. ERSKINE ST & CITY RD, HULME
Incendiary bomb at 6.25 a.m. Fire extinguished. No further report.

168. RUNCORN ST & CORNBROOK ST
H.E. bomb at 6.25 a.m. 23rd. Crater in carriageway in
Runcorn St. Damage to cottage property. Incident closed.

169. CAMDEN GROVE, OFF CEDAR ST, HULME
Reported UXB 7.03 a.m. 23rd. House partly demolished,
but no explosion. Later report no UXB. Incident closed.

170. REPORTED BOOTHS BAKERY. ACTUALLY IN 174 BROWNING ST, COUNTY
[SALFORD, NR TOWN HALL]
Incendiary bomb at 6.25 a.m. 23rd. Fire extinguished
by AFS. Incident closed 9.10 a.m. 23rd.

171. MAYES ST & SHUDEHILL
Joint with incidents Nos 74 & 92.

172. HIGH ST & CHURCH ST [NORTH OF MARKET ST]
Incendiary bomb at 6.30 a.m. 23rd. Extinguished and
incident closed at once. Fire brigade not informed.

173. CHAPEL WALKS & CROSS ST
Incendiary bomb, report says 7.30 a.m. 23rd.
No further information.

175. LOWER CHATHAM ST & DEVONSHIRE ST, C-ON-M
Incendiary bomb at 10.30 p.m. [*sic*] 23rd.
Put out by warden. Incident closed at once.

176. STOCKTON ST, C-ON-M
Incendiary bomb. Report says at 7.45 a.m. 23rd.
No further report.

177. 3 NORTHERN ST, 36. CEDAR ST, HULME
Incendiary bomb during evening of 22nd. Bedroom on
fire. Fire put out and incident closed. No services used.

179. 34 MAPLE ST, HULME
Incendiary bomb during evening of 22nd. Damage to
bedroom. Fire put out by warden. Incident closed.

180. 6 MEADOW ST, STORE ST [OFF GT ANCOATS ST]
UXB reported lying on rubbish heap. H.E. bomb
unexploded later removed and incident closed.

181. OPPOSITE NO. 25 CASTLE ST, KNOTT MILL
UXB reported but later report says this bomb
(H.E.) has exploded. Incident closed.

182. COMMERCIAL MILLS, POMONA
H.E. and incendiary bombs. Also UXB. Attended to by County.

INCIDENTS ARISING FROM ENEMY AIR RAID ON 23RD/24TH DECEMBER 1940

1. CLOPTON ST, TOMLINSON ST, HULME [NORTH OF TOWN HALL]
H.E. dropped 7.45 p.m. in the roadway damaging the
shops 97/99 Clopton St and houses 58 & 57 Tomlinson
St One injured, one dead. Incident still open.

2. 2/6 ARUNDEL ST (APEX) [NEAR ST GEORGE'S CHURCH, CHESTER RD]
H.E. dropped 8.00 p.m. on Messrs. Moorhouse Ltd. building, causing explosion and resultant fire which destroyed the building. One injured. Incident closed 2.15 p.m. 26/12/40 by 'A' Sgt. 12. [These numbers refer to 'A' Division Policemen.]

3. SCHOOL ST, TATTON ST
H.E. presumably dropped but 'A' 235 could find no evidence and closed the incident at 10.55 p.m. 23/12/40.

4. CANNON ST NEAR NEW BROWN ST ON CLEARANCE SITE
Incendiary dropped 8.22 p.m. No damage. Incident closed.

5. ST ANN ST, CROSS ST
Incendiary dropped on building at 8.20 p.m. Fire brigade attended and put out fire. Some damage to building. Incident closed 1.30 a.m. 24/12/40 by 'A' 105.

6. BROWN ST, MARSDEN ST [NEAR SPRING GARDENS]
Incendiary dropped 8.45 p.m. Fire, but soon extinguished. Incident closed 8.55 p.m. 23/12/40 by 'A' 21.

7. BRIDGE ST, WATER ST
H.E. dropped at 8.24 p.m. on building. No fire. Building badly damaged. One slight casualty.
Incident closed 9.21 p.m. 23/12/40 by 'A' Sgt. 13.

8. CORPORATION ST, MARKET ST
Incendiary dropped at 7.18 p.m. Fire resulted. Incident closed at 10.6 p.m. 23/12/40 by 'A' 139. No report of damage.

9. WOODHOUSE'S, DEANSGATE
Incendiary dropped at 8.30 p.m. Serious fire. Damage to building and stock. Incident closed at 10.39 p.m. 28/12/40 by 'A' 261.

10. PEMBERTON'S GARAGE, ATKINSON ST [OFF DEANSGATE]
Incendiary dropped at 8.30 p.m. Slight fire soon extinguished. Incident closed at 8.59 p.m. 23/12/40.

11. RIDGEFIELD – JOHN DALTON ST (FINNIGAN'S)
Incendiary dropped at 8.25 p.m. Slight fire.
Incident closed 9.30 p.m. 23/12/40 by 'A' 190.

12. SOUTH KING ST, RIDGEFIELD [SAME BLOCK AS NO. 11, EAST OF DEANSGATE]
Incendiary dropped at 8.35 p.m. Slight fire causing a little
damage. Incident closed 10.25 p.m. 23/12/40 by 'A' 105.

13. ALBERT HALL, PETER ST
Incendiary dropped at 8.45 p.m. Fire quickly
extinguished. Incident at once closed by 'A' 21.

14. MOSLEY ST, PICCADILLY
Incendiary dropped 9.09 p.m. Fire spread to
Messrs Haslam's buildings etc.; See also incident 29.

15. SPINNINGFIELD, DEANSGATE
Incendiary dropped 8.45 p.m. Fire. Slight damage.
Incident closed 10.41 p.m. 23/12/40 by 'A' 199.

16. 10 CHAPEL WALKS, PALL MALL
Incendiary dropped 9.05 p.m. Fire. Building gutted.
Incident closed 10.35 p.m. 23/12/40 by 'A' 196.

17. DUKE ST, LIVERPOOL ST
[OPPOSITE PRESENT-DAY MUSEUM OF SCIENCE AND INDUSTRY]
H.E. dropped 9.05 p.m. Row of houses damaged.
Five demolished – 35, 39, 41, 43, 51, Duke St.
Incident closed at 9.50 p.m. 23/12/40 by 'A' 219.

18. 40, BRAZENNOSE ST
Incendiary dropped 8.50 p.m. Slight fire quickly
extinguished. Incident closed 11.20 p.m. by 'A' 203.

19. ELLESMERE ST, ARUNDEL ST, CAWDOR ST, HULME
[NORTH OF ST GEORGE'S PARK]
H.E. dropped at approximately 8 p.m. A few
houses demolished. One dead. Incident closed
11.20 p.m. 24/12/40 by 'A' 28.

20. 71, KING ST

Incendiary dropped at 8.55 p.m. Fire. Building damaged. Incident closed 2.15 a.m. 24/12/40 by 'A' 74.

21. ST MARY'S GATE, DEANSGATE

Incendiary dropped at 9.16 p.m. Fire. Extensive damage. Two firemen injured by falling wall. Incident closed 1.08 a.m. 29/12/40.

22. CLARE ST, TEMPLE ST, C-ON-M

H.E. dropped at 10.02 p.m. Nine killed, many injured. 77 & 79 Temple St demolished. Incident closed 9.40 p.m. 25/12/40.

23. HULME HALL RD, CHESTER RD

H.E. & incendiary reported but no trace found. Incident closed 10.50 p.m. 23/12/40.

24. CROSS ST CHAPEL

Incendiary dropped at 10.15 p.m. Fire. Building gutted. Incident closed at 5.50 a.m. 24/12/40 by 'A' 196.

25. ST JAMES SQ.

Incendiary dropped 10.20 p.m. Fire. Building damaged. Incident closed at 24/12/40 [*sic*].

26. LEWIS'S, MARKET ST

Incendiary reported dropped at 10.37 p.m. but no trace was found. Incident closed at 5.15 a.m. 24/12/40.

27. DEANSGATE, ST MARY'S ST

Incendiary reported but no trace found. Incident closed.

28. YORK ST, GEORGE ST

H.E. reported 10.19 p.m. No trace. Incident closed 12.03 a.m. 24/12/40.

29. PARKER ST, GEORGE ST [SEE 32]

H.E. dropped 10.40 p.m. Nine killed, many injured. Large fire caused, building gutted. Incident <u>not</u> closed.

30. CROSS ST, CHAPEL WALKS
Incendiary dropped 10.45 p.m. Not yet closed.

31. SUNKEN SHELTER, TEMPLE ST (WORTHINGTON'S YARD), C-ON-M
H.E, dropped 10.12 p.m. Direct hit on a shelter,
which was vacant. Incident closed 12.25 a.m. 26/12/40.

32. MOSLEY ST, PICCADILLY
See incident 29.

33. SILVER ST, CHORLTON ST [SEE NOS 37,38, 39]
H.E. dropped 11.00 p.m. Large fire resulted.
Eight walking casualties reported. Incident still open.

34. ERSKINE ST, STRETFORD RD
Landmine demolishing much house & shop property.
This was in County area and was handed over to them.

35. OLDHAM ST, PICCADILLY
H.E. reported 11.10 p.m. No further report. Not yet closed.

36. TALBOT HOTEL, STRETFORD RD
Landmine reported, but this is connected with
Incident No. 34. Taken over by County police.

37, MAJOR ST – CHORLTON ST, MAJOR ST –
38, SACKVILLE ST, BLOOM ST – PRINCESS ST
39. Shower of incendiary bombs 11.45 p.m. causing
many destructive fires and linking up with No. 33.
No. 39 misreported. Incident still open.

40. CHETHAM'S COLLEGE
H.E. dropped 11.55 p.m. Roof badly damaged.
Incident closed at 4.35 a.m. 24/12/40.

41. VICTORIA STATION
H.E. dropped at 12.15 a.m. Reported by Inspector of
Railway Police. No further report. Incident closed.

42. 36 John Dalton St

Incendiary dropped at 11.50 p.m. Fire. Damage to
building. Incident closed 1.30 a.m. 24/12/40 by 'A' 187.

43. Albert Bridge, Water St, Bridge St

H.E. This incident is connected with incident No. 7,
and should be closed with that incident.

44. 37 Hazel St, off Bedford St [NW of Hulme Town Hall]

UXB H.E. Dropped at approx. midnight. Tenants of
adjacent property evacuated to Milton Hall. [Deansgate]
Incident closed at 2.52 p.m. 24/12/40 by 'A' 129.

45. Spencer St, City Rd [west of Gaythorn Gasworks]

Incendiary bomb dropped at 2.30 a.m. 24/12/40.
Fire broke out. No report of any damage. Incident closed.

46. Swan Lane, New Brown St [north of Market St]

Incendiary dropped 3.00 a.m. 24/12/40.
Extensive fire, buildings gutted. Incident still open.

47. Town Hall, Princess St end

Incendiary dropped 8.00 p.m. Fire. Water on every floor.
No further report. Incident still open.

48. Jackson St, City Rd (Trades Supply Co.)

H.E. dropped 9.45 p.m. Damage to building.
Incident closed at 7.49 a.m. 24/12/40 by 'A' 286.

49. Arch 32, Hulme Locks [short branch canal linking
Bridgewater Canal with River Irwell]

H.E. dropped 9.20 p.m. Two dead. Incident closed
3.35 p.m. 24/12/40 by 'A' 304.

50. 17 Bright St, City Rd [east of St George's Park, Hulme]

Incendiary dropped during evening of 23/12/40.
Roof collapsed at 10.24 a.m. 24/12/40. Incident still open.

51. MARSHALL SIDE WAREHOUSE, WATER ST

H.E. reported unexploded had exploded. Warehouse damaged.
Incident closed 1.24 a.m. 24/12/40 by 'A' Sergeant 36.

52. LEAF ST, CATON ST, HULME

H.E. dropped 9.30 p.m. Two dead, two houses demolished.
Incident closed 3.30 p.m. 26/12/40 by 'A' 226.

A full list of those civilians killed or injured in Manchester and Salford during the Luftwaffe attacks throughout the Second World War is given in Peter Smith's excellent book Luftwaffe Over Manchester. *Also see pages 21–29 in* Memories of the Salford Blitz *– see bibliography. The Stretford list of casualties is also available from Trafford Archives, Sale Library.*

A memorial to the Manchester civilian dead, Southern Cemetery. *(Author's collection)*

APPENDIX 2

STRETFORD BOMBING INCIDENTS 22–24 DECEMBER 1940

I.B. = Incendiary Bomb
H.E. = High-Explosive Bomb
L.M. = Landmine (Parachute Mine)
UXB = Unexploded Bomb
A.A. = Anti-aircraft
Dem = Property Demolished
Ev = Evacuated
B.B. = Bomb Blast
GMF = Greater Manchester Fire Brigade dealt with the incident
AFS = Auxiliary Fire Service

22ND DECEMBER:

Cromwell Road, Marston Road, & Longford Park	I.B.s
Junc, Buckingham Road, near Girls' High School	I.B.
Colley Street	I.B.
10 Gorse Street	I.B.
Corrugated Paper Works, Ayres Road	I.B.
Quicks Garage, Chester Road	I.B.
Grammar School	I.B.
Welsh Chapel, Chorlton Road	I.B.
53 Premier Street	I.B.
28 Hornby Street	I.B.
Albion Street	I.B.
53 Milner Street	I.B.
Reynolds Road	I.B.

Mosaic Works, Blackburn Street	I.B.
Harper Street	I.B.
Henshaws Blind Inst, Chester Road	I.B.
Royston Road (Dem)	H.E.
Kings Road near Railway Bridge (Dem)	H.E.
Globe Cinema & Savilles	I.B.
Hawkens Street	I.B.
Lostock Estate	Flares
Junc, Shrewsbury Street and Stamford Street	I.B.
Crofton Street behind Bracegirdles	I.B.
Garage, Walter Street	I.B.
Opposite No 14 Post, Kings Road	H.E. & 2 UXB
114 Humphrey Road	I.B.
57 Milton Road (2 houses Dem, 40 people Ev)	H.E.
Near Stretford Garage, Chester Road	I.B.
Opposite Venos, Chester Road	I.B.
Cowley and Radivans Garage, Chester Road	I.B.
Clifton Street opposite St Bride's church	H.E.
Oxford Street	H.E.
Stretford Road, opposite East Union Street	I.B.
Northleigh Road (houses Dem)	H.E.
Gasworks	I.B.
Kings Road Railway Bridge	I.B.
Tamworth Street	H.E.
497 Stretford Road	I.B.
Hare Motors Co.	UXB (suspected)
Ship Canal Cricket Ground	I.B.
Metrovicks Club	I.B.
27 Nansen Street	I.B.
Goods Yard C.L.R.	H.E.

149 Duke Street	H.E.
Crofton Street	H.E.
Balloon Site, 16 Royal Avenue	UXB × 2
Henrietta Street	H.E.
Shrewsbury Street	H.E. & I.B.
201 Kings Road	H.E.
Trafalgar Square	I.B.
739 Chester Road	I.B.
Near Dog & Partridge, Chester Road	I.B.
Opposite Henshaw's Institute for the Blind	H.E. (UXB)
Ryebank Road	I.B.
St Peter's church	H.E.
Bradshaws field, Davyhulme Road	I.B. × 12
1 Grange Avenue	I.B.
Darnley Street	I.B.
98/104 Humphrey Road	H.E.
Bold Street and Clarence Street corner	I.B.
Clarence Street near St Joseph's School	I.B.
47 Hadfield Street	L.M. UX
Thorpe Yard, Wright Street	I.B.
Unitarian church, Shrewsbury Street	I.B.
Opposite Cowans, Chester Road	I.B.
Arthur Street	I.B.
Coleridge Road & Wordsworth Road corner	H.E.
Auburn Road & Kings Road corner	H.E.
Yeadon & Taylor, Cornbrook Park Road	I.B.
4 Derbyshire Lane	I.B.
Virgil Street	I.B.
42 & 104 Norwood Road	I.B.s
131 Kings Road (House Dem)	H.E.

AFS Fire Station, Talbot Road	UXB & A.A. shell
Chester Road near Great Stone Road	B.B.
118 Ryebank Road (250 Ev)	UXB
Borough Billposting Co., Chester Road	I.B.
Wellington Crescent	Phone wires down
32 Strathmere Avenue	I.B.
Evans Bellhouse, City Road	I.B.
Dragon Garage, Chester Road	UXB
Addison Crescent and Lime Crescent corner (Houses Dem)	H.E.

23RD DECEMBER (A.M.):

Addison Crescent and Ruthen Lane corner	H.E.
28 Upper Chorlton Road	H.E.
66 Gorse Crescent	H.E.
79 Oxford Street	H.E.
Basement of Henshaw's Inst. for the Blind	UXB
Victoria Park	B.B.
City Road and Chester Road corner	H.E.
Clifton Street	H.E. × 2
35, 48/50 Auburn Road	H.E.
384 Kings Road	H.E.
131, 133 Kings Road	H.E.
71 Duke Street	H.E.
Stuart Road	B.B.
95 Gorse Crescent	H.E.
Lostock Estate	flares
6, 8 Dalton Avenue	H.E.
49 Thornbury Road	I.B.
Norton Street (gas main on fire)	H.E.
Seymour Garage	H.E. blast

Duke Street	H.E.
NW Stretford	flares
Oxford Street & Elton Street	H.E.
Stanley Road and Henrietta Street	H.E.
15, 17 Curzon Street	H.E.
Norton Street	H.E.
Junc, Kings Road and Milner Street (GMF)	H.E.
Northleigh Road	I.B.s × 10
Field near Sandy Lane	H.E.
57 Norton Street	H.E.
Henshaw's Inst.	I.B.
Ryebank Road & Erlington Avenue	I.B.s × 6
Milwain Road Shelter	H.E.
Oakfield Road & Blenheim Road	H.E. × 2
Kings Road & Knutsford Avenue (GMF)	H.E.
Rear of Thirlmere Avenue	UXB
38 Ryebank Road (water main burst)	H.E.
Cornbrook Street	I.B.
80 Stamford Street	H.E.
Trafford Park Station (GMF)	H.E.
AFS Station, Milner Street	UXB
9 Lindow Road	H.E.
11 Milwain Road (rear)	H.E.
Kings Road/Ashley Avenue	H.E.
Hornby Road	H.E.
Police Station, East Union Street *[6 policemen killed]* *[The typewritten Archive gives Entwistle Street here, but this is almost certainly a transcription error.]*	H.E.
Urmston Lane	I.B.
Field rear of Dalton Avenue	H.E. × 2

Trafford Wharf	H.E.
Flat attached to Longford Cinema	H.E.
15, 18 Lime Road	I.B.
25 Westwood Road	H.E. UXB
Park Road near Kellogg's	H.E. UXB
Bridge Inn, Stretford	I.B.
Chester Road near Northumberland Hotel	H.E.
Westbourne Road (rear of No. 4)	H.E.
16 Thirlmere Avenue	H.E.
Rees Oils, Trafford Park	I.B.
Metrovicks, Mosley Road	L.M. UXB
Stamford Street	H.E. × 2
Wilton Avenue (200 Ev)	L.M. UXB
Buckingham Road & Railway Road on Railway Line	L.M.
23 Burleigh Road (6 houses on fire)	I.B.
Chester Road, 50yds from Eye Platt Bridge	H.E.
Junc, St John's Road & Chorlton Road (9 Houses Dem)	L.M.
27 Woodstock Road (7 people trapped)	H.E.
105 Gorse Crescent	UXB
95 Gorse Crescent	H.E.
Park Road near Railway Bridge	H.E.
Yeadon and Taylor, Cornbrook	L.M. UXB
25 Virgil Street (Main Sewer)	L.M.
Nadins Farm, Old Hall Road	H.E.
25yds from Signal Box, Old Trafford	L.M. UXB
6 Darwen Street	L.M.
Field near Urmston boundary	H.E. × 6
Norbury Printers, Elsinore Road	UXB
Open Air School	I.B.s × 3

23RD/24TH DECEMBER:

Town Hall (2 injured)	H.E.
37 Melville Road	I.B.
Park Road & Derbyshire Lane. Fire	I.B.
Empty house behind Derbyshire Avenue. Fire	I.B.
31 Marlborough Road	I.B.
Between Lostock Library & Melville Road Gas main damaged	I.B.s × 40
Kelloggs (Park Road blocked)	H.E.
Park Road Post Office	H.E.
147 Derbyshire Lane (back of house blown out)	H.E.
178, 183 Urmston Lane (Dem)	H.E.
Radstock Road	I.B.s × 6
9, 11 Raglan Road	H.E.
3 Leyburn Avenue	H.E.
Derbyshire Grove	H.E.
1, 3 Colwell Avenue	H.E.
364, 366 Barlow Road (200 Ev)	UXB
St. George's Road and Urmston Lane corner	H.E.
Between Lostock Bridge & Curzon Road	H.E. × 7
Labour Exchange, Brunswick Street	H.E.
Land behind Highfield Road [SW of Cemetery]	H.E.
Junc, Sandy Lane & Urmston Lane	H.E.
279, 281 Derbyshire Lane West	H.E.
School shelter Victoria Park School	H.E. × 2
Victoria Park playing fields	H.E. × 3
22/28 Braemar Avenue	H.E.
92/114 Victoria Road	H.E. & I.B.
Thirlmere Avenue	I.B.
Metrovicks Club	I.B.

37/43 Arlington Road	H.E.
462 Barton Road (Warden collapsed)	
All Saints church, Cyprus Street	I.B.
1 Braemar Avenue	H.E.
78 Cromwell Road (water main)	H.E.
Stanley Road *[33 killed]*	L.M.
Davyhulme Road & Coniston Road	L.M.
Raglan Road & Melville Road	L.M.
Globe Theatre *[Cinema]*	H.E.
Gasworks, Longford Road	H.E.
Grange Avenue, house and garage	I.B.s × 4
109 Braemar Avenue	H.E.
Essex Street	H.E.
69 Milton Road	H.E.
Girls' High School and surrounding houses	L.M.
Ponsonby Road & Haigh Road	H.E.
13 Barkway Road (150 Ev)	UXB
Lostock School	I.B.
Carriage Street (gas main)	H.E.
1 Winster Avenue (100 Ev)	UXB
85 Chatsworth Road	H.E.
Gorse Crescent	H.E.
Thorpe Street, several fires	I.B.
347 Barton Road. Fire	I.B.
White City *[greyhound stadium]*	L.M. UXB
Railway, back of Derbyshire Avenue	UXB
Dalton Avenue	H.E. × 2
97 School Road	H.E.
8 Mona Avenue	I.B. UXB
79 Moss Road	H.E.

18 Radstock Road	H.E. UXB
Romiley Road, Davyhulme	H.E.
Sewage Farm *[north of River Mersey]* (People Ev)	UXB × 2
Rear of Anderson & Son Ltd, Park Road/ Bridgewater Canal	H.E. × 2
Hancocks Farm, Park Road	H.E. × 4
Between Kellogg's and Bridgewater Canal	H.E.
Wharf Road	UXB
165 Tamworth Street	H.E.
Eye Platt Bridge *[on Chester Rd, 600 yds north of Crossford Bridge]*	UXB
Fisher Renwicks, Cornbrook	UXB
87 Hadfield Street	UXB
Cornbrook Sidings	H.E.
Railway Line, end of Turner Street *[opposite Pomona Docks]*	H.E.

Memorial to the Stretford civilian dead in Stretford Cemetery. *(Author's collection)*

APPENDIX 3

SALFORD BOMBING INCIDENTS SEPTEMBER 1940 – JUNE 1941

4–5 Sep 1940		23.37 until 04.24		MESSAGES	21
15 HE, 1 UXB, 2 oil bombs				FIRES	1 serious
KILLED	2	SERIOUSLY WOUNDED	11	SLIGHTLY WOUNDED	36
Bombs at Berry Wiggins, Old People's Home, Victoria Road					

2–3 Oct 1940		22.42 until 00.58		MESSAGES	72
9 HE, 3 UXB, 5 oil bombs				FIRES	0
KILLED	3	SERIOUSLY WOUNDED	2	SLIGHTLY WOUNDED	0

7–8 Oct 1940		20.34 until 00.15		MESSAGES	78
150/200kg incendiaries				FIRES	3 serious
KILLED	0	SERIOUSLY WOUNDED	0	SLIGHTLY WOUNDED	0

11 Oct 1940		00.28 until 04.12		MESSAGES	85
1 HE, 2 oil bombs, 100kg incendiaries				FIRES	0
KILLED	0	SERIOUSLY WOUNDED	0	SLIGHTLY WOUNDED	10
Albert Park Library destroyed 03.55					

22–24 Dec 1940		–	MESSAGES	175+
220-250 HE, 51 UXB, 26 mines, 7,000-10,000 incendiaries			FIRES	32 serious
KILLED	197	SERIOUSLY WOUNDED 177	SLIGHTLY WOUNDED	648
'Blitz'; casualty figures exclude 12 missing				

9 Jan 1941	19.40 until 01.21	MESSAGES	191
10 HE, 100kg incendiaries		FIRES	0
KILLED 0	SERIOUSLY WOUNDED 2	SLIGHTLY WOUNDED	10
Broughton and Seedley districts at 20.15			

11 Mar 1941	20.47 until 23.51	MESSAGES	214
30 HE, 9 UXB, 500kg incendiaries		FIRES	2 serious
KILLED 11	SERIOUSLY WOUNDED 79	SLIGHTLY WOUNDED	27
Bombs at docks (3 ships), Ladywell and Hope Hospitals, Eccles New Road flats			

15 April 1941	21.42 until 04.07	MESSAGES	236
4 HE		FIRES	0
KILLED 2	SERIOUSLY WOUNDED 9	SLIGHTLY WOUNDED	15
Laundry Street, Littleton Road, Grecian Street, at 00.20			

7 May 1941	23.52 until 04.13	MESSAGES	251
35 HE, 2 UXB, 200–300kg incendiaries		FIRES	0
KILLED 3	SERIOUSLY WOUNDED 8	SLIGHTLY WOUNDED	31
Pendleton and Higher Broughton Districts			

2 June 1941	00.37 until 03.19	**MESSAGES**	268
70 HE, 5 UXB, 4 oil bombs, 1,500kg incendiaries		**FIRES**	0
KILLED 43	**SERIOUSLY WOUNDED** 37	**SLIGHTLY WOUNDED**	102
Damage to Salford Royal Hospital			

The memorial to Salford civilian war dead in Agecroft Cemetery. *(Author's collection)*

APPENDIX 4

MANCHESTER REST CENTRES DURING THE BLITZ

The original numbered list was compiled on 27 September 1940. Also included are those premises in use later, some of them infrequently, as overflow from nearby Rest Centres. Estimated capacity of number of possible users is given where stated by the ECM.

1	Brookfield church Sunday school, Hyde Road, Gorton	500
2	St Stephen's Sunday school, Conran Street, Harpurhey	800
3	Methodist Sunday school, South Street, Longsight	500
4	Zion Institute, Stretford Road, Hulme	700
5	Trinity Presbyterian Sunday school, Cheetham Hill Road	200
6	Blackley Methodist Schools, Ward Street	400
7	Newton Heath Town Hall	400
8	Assembly Rooms, 109 Cheetham Hill Road	100
9	Brooke Street, Bradford	200
10	United Methodist church, Whitworth Street, Openshaw	300
11	St Edmund's Parish Hall, Alexandra Road, Moss Side	400
12	Platt Parish Hall, Rusholme	300
13	Levenshulme Town Hall, Stockport Road	400

14	Withington Town Hall, Lapwing Lane, West Didsbury	300
15	St Matthew's Sunday school, Cleveland Road, Crumpsall	500
16	All Souls' Sunday school, Every Street, Ancoats	200
17	St Saviour's Sunday school, Plymouth Grove, Chorlton-on-Medlock	200
18	Methodist Sunday school, High Lane, Chorlton-cum-Hardy	200
19	St Paul's Sunday school, Chapel Street, Didsbury	600
20	St Luke's church hall, Brownley Road, Wythenshawe	200
Later additions:		
St Luke's and Christ Church Sunday school, Burton Road, Withington		100
St Paul's Sunday school, Chapel Street, Didsbury		100
Church Rooms, Kenworthy Lane, Northenden		100
Scouts Hall, Avon Road, Burnage		100
Ardwick Lads' Club, Palmerston Street		200
Girls' Institute, Mill Street, Ancoats		200
Wood Street Mission, off Deansgate		300
Milton Hall, Deansgate		250
McLaren Baptist School, Sibson Road, Chorlton-cum-Hardy		60 *[overflow from 18 on 24/12/40]*
St Luke's Sunday school, Chorlton-on-Medlock		30 *[overflow from 17 on 24/12/40]*

Maximum 2 nights, over Christmas Blitz 1940:
Carlton Cinema, Seymour Road, Clayton
Carver Hall, Clayton
Seymour Road Schools, Clayton
Cavendish Street School, Chorlton-on-Medlock

THE LIST OF 'FIRST LINE' REST CENTRES AS AT 18 SEPTEMBER 1941 (SIXTY-FIVE IN ALL), NOT INCLUDING THOSE MENTIONED ABOVE, WAS AS FOLLOWS:

Whalley Range Methodist Sunday school, Withington Road	100
Roby Congregational Sunday school, Dickenson Road	175
Wesley Street Methodist Sunday school, Levenshulme	150
Hopkinson Road Methodist Sunday school, Higher Blackley	75
Platt Lane Methodist Sunday school, Rusholme	100
Ashley Lane Methodist Sunday school, Moston	150
Elm Street Methodist Sunday school, Miles Platting	100
Moss Side Baptist church and school	100
Hope Hall, Brunswick Street, Chorlton-on-Medlock	75
Queen's Park Congregational church, Rochdale Road	100
Beech Mount Methodist Sunday school, Harpurhey	200
Wellington Street Baptist School, Gorton	150
Crab Lane Methodist Sunday school, Higher Blackley	100
MacFayden Memorial Sunday school, Barlow Moor Road, Chorlton-cum-Hardy	150
New Islington Public Hall, Ancoats	150
Wilmslow Road Methodist Sunday school, Withington	100

Grey Mare Lane Methodist Sunday school, Lower Openshaw	150
Aspinal Methodist Sunday school, Reddish Lane, Gorton	100
Chancery Lane Methodist Sunday school, Ardwick	150
Ancoats Lads' Club, Spectator Street, Beswick	100
Chain Bar Methodist Sunday school, Moston Lane	70
Bridgewater Hall, Silver Street, Hulme	150
Blackley Institute, Tudor Avenue, Blackley	100
Burnage Congregational School	200
Crossley Lads' Club, Ashton Old Road, Openshaw	200
Charter Street Institute, Dantzic Street	200
Cheetham Public Hall, Cheetham Hill Road	100
Churnet Street Public Hall, Collyhurst	100
Hugh Oldham Lads' Club, Livesey Street, Collyhurst	200
Ivy Cottage Mission, 97 Barlow Moor Road, Didsbury	60
Lower Mosley Street School, City	200
Church Street Methodist Sunday school, Beswick	150
South Street Methodist Sunday school, Longsight	75
McLaren Memorial Sunday school, Eileen Grove, Rusholme	100
Manchester University, Oxford Road	200
Platt Parish Hall, Rusholme	75
Royal Oak Centre, Wythenshawe	100
Seymour Road Congregational church, Clayton	150
St Mary's Road School, Newton Heath	200
Palatine Road Congregational church, Withington	100
Simpson Memorial Institute, Moston Lane	100
Whitworth Art Gallery, Whitworth Park	200

Cheetham Women's institute, Cheetham Hill Road	200
Birch Street Baptist Sunday school, Gorton	100
St Clement's School, Higher Openshaw	100

COMPANIES INVOLVED IN SUPPLYING FOOD TO REST CENTRES:

CWS Manchester and Salford	51 Downing Street, Ardwick
Duncan and Fosters	102 York Street, C-on-Med
Smallmans	Heald Grove, Rusholme
Agars	30 Wilbraham Road, Fallowfield
Robinson and Smith	Bank Street, Levenshulme
UCP	Russell Street, Levenshulme

All food and drink was free of charge to *bona fide* homeless in Rest Centres. The council was obliged to fulfil all debts to food suppliers within seven days.

APPENDIX 5

STRETFORD REST CENTRES DURING THE BLITZ

Barton Road Independent Methodist Chapel
Edge Lane Union Chapel
Gorse Hill Methodist Chapel
Public Hall, Chester Road
Junior Boys' School, Stretford Road, Old Trafford

The above was the list at May 1941.
The next year the following were added:

Old Trafford Institute, Stretford Road
Seymour Park Senior Girls' School, Northumberland Road,
Old Trafford
Gorse Park School, Gorse Hill
Trades and Labour Club, Chester Road
Congregational School, South Croston Street, Old Trafford
Congregational School, Chester Road

Trafford Park Industrial Estate had two Rest Centres, apart from the
facilities provided by the major firms, e.g. Metrovicks – see text.

St Antony's, Eleventh Street
St Cuthbert's, Third Avenue

LUFTWAFFE RECONNAISSANCE MAPS: SALFORD DOCKS AREA

Two overlapping portions of a larger map from August 1940 are shown overleaf (from Trafford Archives). The original A2 sheet shows the whole of Trafford Park to the west, and as far as Chorlton-on-Medlock to the east. Numbered targets – those of especial interest to the bombers – were printed alongside the map:

83 Eisenbahnbrücke über den Irwell Fluß

101 Straßenbrücke über den Irwell Fluß und den Manchester Ship-Canal (Bild)

196 *(not shown on this map)* Metropolitan Vickers El. Co. Ltd in Manchester-Trafford Park (Bild)

200 R. u. W. Paul, Futtermittelfabrik an den Pomona Docks in Manchester-Salford

201 4 Pomona Docks zusammen 9,3 ha Wasserfläche, 1794 m Kailänge, 7 m Tiefe, 457 Breite; für Seeschiffe bis 5 m Tiefgang

202 4 Salford Docks zusammen 9,3 ha Wasserfläche, 4139 m Kailänge, 8,5 m Wassertiefe, 68,5 m bis 76,2 Einfahrtsbreite; Überseeverkehr mit großen Schiffen, Trafford Kai und Salford Kai (Frachtverkehr, Getreideumschlag, Großsilo) (Bild)

203 3 Mode Wheel Trockendocks in Manchester-Salfords für leichte Kreuzer und Zerstörer

204 Schwimmdock der Manchester Dry Docks Co. Ltd in Manchester-Salford für U-Bote und Minensucher

205 Bleiwerk in Manchester-Salford

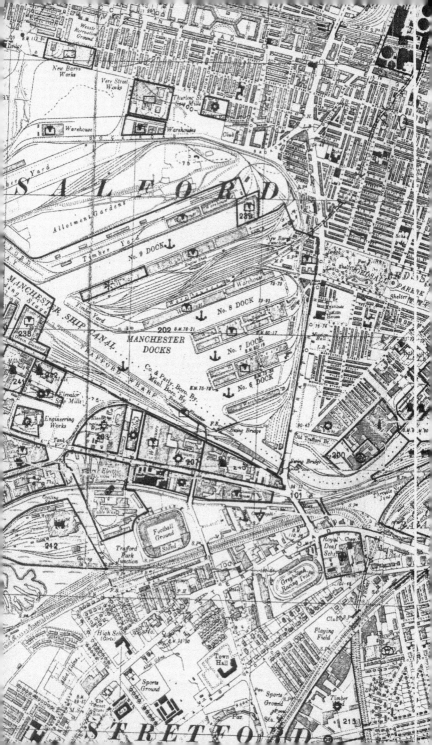

GLOSSARY

Abstellgleise	railway sidings
Bauart	construction
Bild	picture
Bleiwerk	lead works
Breite	width
Brücke	bridge
Eisenbahn	railway
Futtermittelfabrik	food-processing plant
Frachtverkehr	cargo traffic
Getredeumschlag	grain silo
Güterbahnhof	railway goods station
Holzplatz	timber yard
Kailange	quay length
Kanalscheusen	canal locks
Kohlenschuppen	coal sheds
Kraftwerk	power station
Kreuzer	cruisers
Lagerhäuser	warehouses
Minensucher	minesweeper
Mühle	mill
Ölmühle	oil mill
Schwimmdock	floating dock
Straßenbrücke	road bridge
südlich vom	(to the) south of
Südufer	southern bank
Tiefe	depth
Trockendocks	dry dock
Überseeverkehr	shipping, sea traffic
Verschiebebahnhof	planned railway station
Viehhof	cattle farm
Zentralbahnhof	Central Station
Zerstörer	destroyers
zusammen	together
zwischen	between

APPENDIX 7

SALFORD REST CENTRES DURING THE BLITZ

Broughton Union Church School, Moss Street
Mount Street School
Stowell Memorial School, School Street
Hope Congregational School, Liverpool Street
Regent Road Methodist School
Public Assistance Offices, Town Hall, Police Street, Pendleton
Independent Methodist School, Fitzwarren Street, Seedley
Weaste Congregational School, Weaste Road

APPENDIX 8

MANCHESTER AND SALFORD BOMBING MAPS

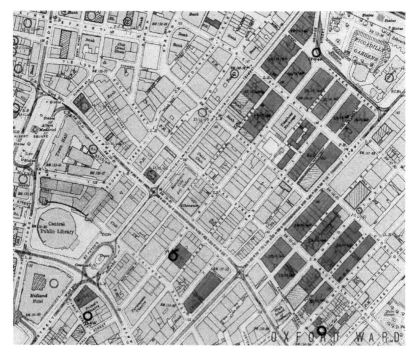

A major feature of this map is the severely hit warehouse district on either side of Portland Street. The Bradford Dyers' Association factory, the trapezoid shape immediately to the south of St Peter's Square and the Central Library, was also gutted. (See Chapter Four for more details.) Alongside is the Midland Hotel, which was to have been Hitler's residence in Manchester had the invasion been successful. Hitler wanted it preserved undamaged, which is possibly why just the one incendiary bomb – soon extinguished – is recorded as having fallen there.

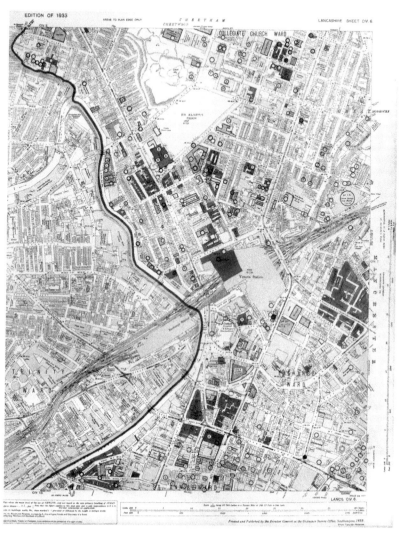

From the south, moving north-east: warehouses alongside the Irwell were targeted, and the fires spread around the Albert Street and Bridge Street area. Towards the cathedral, the triangular block of the Victoria Buildings is clear, as are the rectangle of the Royal Exchange and the axe-head shape of the Cotton Exchange block. To the east of Victoria Station the office and commercial area, which contained Baxendale's on Miller Street, is highlighted. North of Victoria Station, amongst the buildings destroyed were the Assize Courts on the south-west corner of the prison, and the blocks of shops along Bury New Road.

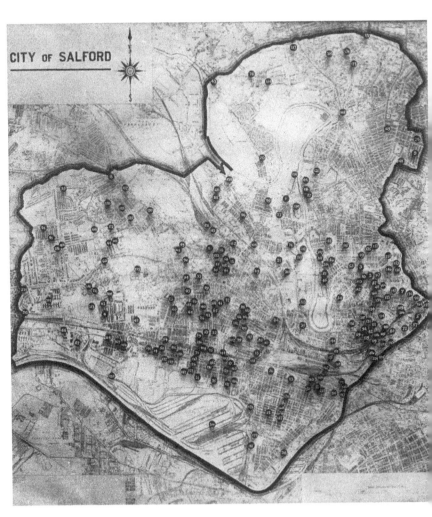

CITY OF SALFORD

This map records the bombs dropped on Salford during the 1940 Christmas Blitz.
The sheer number of incidents, and the widespread attack on civilian areas, are the two
most salient aspects of this map. See Chapter Five for more precise details.

APPENDIX 9

ANTI-AIRCRAFT PLACEMENTS AROUND MANCHESTER IN THE SECOND WORLD WAR

PLACEMENT	GRID REFERENCE (OS Landranger Map 109)
Heaton Park	834037
Broadhurst Park, Moston	880024
Manchester Central, Great Horrocks	848003
Manchester Central, Smedley Junction	851006
Guide Bridge	922 964
Little Moss	915001
Melland playing fields, Levenshulme	885948
Melland playing fields, Levenshulme	888948
Hough End Fields	831934
Turn Moss, Chorlton-cum-Hardy	806937
Barton Dock Road, Lostock	772958
Peel Green, north of Barton Aerodrome	747979
Ellesmere Park	778999
Peel Park, Salford	821993
Irlams o' th' Height (Park Lane Farm)	801011
Middleton	859055
Brookdale	890015

Medlock Vale	899000
Ashton-under-Lyne	913977
Birchfields Park	858948
University playing fields (Birchfields Road)	862942
Ellesmere Golf Course, Roe Green	748022
Woodley playing fields	929921
Ackers Farm, Carrington Lane	756927
Moorside Road Sports Ground, Davyhulme	761950
Davyhulme Park	748954
Botany Bay Wood (east of), Eccles	736984
Westwood Park, Worsley	753993
Grimshaw playing field, Prestwich	817040
Whitefield Golf Course	801053
Morley Green, south of Ringway Airport	820826
Wythenshawe Park	808900
Green Lane Sports Ground, Heaton Norris	879910

BIBLIOGRAPHY AND SOURCES

Abram, Jake, *Tugs, Barges and Me: Manchester Ship Canal and Bridgewater Canal Memories* (Neil Richardson, 1996)

Atherton, J.G., *Home to Stay: Stretford in the Second World War* (Neil Richardson, 1991)

Birchall, Johnston, *Co-op: The People's Business* (Manchester University Press, 1994)

Bonner, Robert F., *Manchester Fire Brigade* (Archive Publications, 1988)

Broady, Duncan, and Sawkill, Carol, *The Police! 150 Years of Policing in the Manchester Area* (Archive Publications, 1989)

Clayton, David, *Manchester Stories* (pp. 27-36), (Fort Publishing Ltd, 2013)

Coggins, David, *Manchester: The Cathedral in the Blitz* (duologue for recital, 1990)

Cooper, Ian, Hardy, Clive, and Hochland, Henry, *Manchester at War: A Pictorial Account 1939-45* (*MEN* Special Edition) (Archive Productions Ltd, 1986)

Corrigan, Matthew, *The Manchester Heinkel* (Caliver Books, 2013)

Davies, Fred, *My Father's Eyes: Episodes in the Life of a Hulme Man* (Neil Richardson, 1985)

Deakin, Derick, *Wythenshawe: The Story of a Garden City* (pp. 87-93) (Phillimore, 1986)

Dobinson, Colin, *AA Command: Britain's Anti-Aircraft Defences of World War Two* (Methuen, 2001)

Dobkin, Monty, *More Tales of Manchester Jewry* (Neil Richardson, 1994)

Dummelow, John, *Metropolitan-Vickers Electrical Company Ltd 1899-1949* (Metrovicks Manchester, 1949)

Eccles Library Writers, *Tall Tales and Short Stories of the Manchester Ship Canal 1894-1994* (Eccles Library Writers, 2013)

Eccles Library Writers, *Workshop of the World: 100 Years of Trafford Park* (Eccles Library Writers, 2013)

Fleischer, Wolfgang, *German Air-dropped Weapons to 1945* (Midland Publishing, 2006)

Forrest, Sharon, and Wyke, Terry, *Zion 100: A History of a Building in Hulme* (Zion Arts Centre, 2011)

France, Ernest, *A History of Gorton and Openshaw* (E. France, 1989)

Freethy, Ron, *Cheshire: The Secret War 1939-45* (Countryside Books, 2012)

Freethy, Ron, *Lancashire: The Secret War 1939-45* (Countryside Books, 2009)

Freethy, Ron, *Lancashire v. Hitler: Civilians at War* (Countryside Books, 2006)

Galland, A., Ries, K., and Ahnert, R., (Tr. I. and D. Dunbar; Ed. Mondey, David) *The Luftwaffe at War 1939-45* (Ian Allan, 1972)

Gardiner, Juliet, *The Blitz: The British under Attack* (HarperPress, 2010)

Garside, Pam, and Breen, Lesley (ed.), *Greater Manchester 125 Years: Images from the Manchester Evening News* (Breedon, 1993)

Hall, Susan, *Workhouses and Hospitals of North Manchester* (Neil Richardson, 2004)

Hardy, Clive, *Manchester at War* (First Edition/*MEN*, 2005)

Hayes, Cliff (ed.), *Our Blitz: Red Sky Over Manchester* (Kemsley Newspapers Ltd, 1945)

Hayes, Cliff and Sylvia, *Britain in Old Photographs: Stretford* (Sutton Publishing, 1997)

Heaton, Frank: *The Manchester Village: Deansgate Remembered* (Neil Richardson, 1995)

Hennell, Michael, *The Deans and Canons of Manchester Cathedral 1840–1948* (Chetham's Library, 1984)

Holland, James, *The Battle of Britain* (Corgi, 2011)

Howarth, Ken, *Manchester Wartime Memories* (Manchester Library and Information Services, 2006)

Hylton, Stuart, *A History of Manchester* (Phillimore, 2010)

Hylton, Stuart, *Reporting the Blitz: News from the Home Front Communities* (The History Press, 2012)

Jones, Steve, *When the Lights Went Down: Crime in Wartime London and Manchester* (Wicked Publications, 2000)

Jordan, Mary, *Hulme Memories* (Neil Richardson, 1989)

Keegan, John, *A History of Warfare* (pp. 366-375) (Random House, 1993)

Knibb, Kathleen, *An Epitaph for a Bygone Manchester* (pp. 63-66) (Kathleen Knibb, 1993)

Lavery, Brian, *The British Home Front Pocket-Book* (Conway, 2010)

Levine, Joshua, *Forgotten Voices of the Blitz and the Battle for Britain: A New History in the Words of the Men and Women on Both Sides* (Random House/Imperial War Museum, 2006)

Line, Paul Leslie, *A Guide to Manchester 1927* (Collins Bartholomew, 2011)

Makepeace, Chris, *A Century of Manchester* (Sutton Publishing, 1999)

Masterson, Vicki, and Cliff, Karen, *Stretford: An Illustrated History* (Breedon, 2002)

Newhill, John P., *50 Years of Change: The Story of Procter and Gamble Ltd in Trafford Park* (Procter and Gamble, 1984)

Nicholls, Robert, *The Belle Vue Story* (Neil Richardson, 1992)

Nicholls, Robert, *Trafford Park: The First 100 Years* (Phillimore, 1996)

Overy, Richard, *The Bombing War: Europe 1939–45* (Allen Lane, 2013)

Pegg, Eric, *Lower Broughton Remembered* (pp. 13-28) (Neil Richardson, 1997)

Phythian, Graham, *Manchester at War 1939–45: The People's Story* (The History Press, 2014)

Phythian, Graham, *South Manchester Remembered* (The History Press, 2012)

Potts, Bob, *The Old Pubs of Hulme and Chorlton-on-Medlock* (Neil Richardson, 1983)

Potts, Bob, *The Old Pubs of Rochdale Road and Neighbourhood Manchester* (Neil Richardson, 1985)

Rea, Anthony, *Manchester's Little Italy: Memories of the Italian Colony of Ancoats* (pp. 38-9) (Neil Richardson, 1988)

Rowlinson, Frank, *Contribution To Victory: An account of the special work of the Metropolitan-Vickers Electrical Company Limited in the Second World War* (Metrovicks, 1947)

Saunders, Hilary Saint George, *Ford at War* (Ford, 1946)

Shaw, Frank and Joan, *We Remember the Blitz* (Ebury Press, 2012)

Smith, Peter J.C., *Flying Bombs Over the Pennines* (Neil Richardson, 1988)

Smith, Peter J.C., *Luftwaffe Over Manchester, The Blitz Years 1940–44* (Neil Richardson, 2003)

Stern, Joseph Peter, *Hitler, The Führer and The People* (Collins, 1975)

Stevens, T.H.G., *Some Notes on the Development of Trafford Park* (Trafford Park Estates, 1947)

Süss, Dietmar, (Tr. Lesley Sharpe and Jeremy Noakes) *Death from the Skies: How the British and Germans Survived Bombing in World War II [Tod aus der Luft: Kriegsgesellschaft und Luftkrieg in Deutschland und England]* (Oxford University Press, 2014)

Thomas, Pete, and Drum, Neil, *Two Towns go to War: Irlam and Cadishead's part in the Second World War 1939–1945 (Vol.1)* (Thomas-Drum Publications 2014)

Upton, Dennis, 'Flying Bombs over Yorkshire', *Yorkshire Ridings Magazine* Oct/Nov 1987, pp. 45-47

Various, *Front Line 1940–41: The Official Story of the Civil Defence of Britain* (HM Stationery Office, 1942)

Various, *Kelloggs: Fifty Years of Making Sunshine 1938–88* (Kelloggs, 1988)

Walsh, Frank, *From Hulme to Eternity* (Walsh, 2007)

Warrender, Keith, *Below Manchester* (Willow Publishing, 2009)

Warrender, Keith, *Underground Manchester* (Willow Publishing, 2007/2012)

Watson, Barbara, *Irlams o' th' Height: The Growth and Destruction of a Village 1600–1987* (Neil Richardson 1987)

Wheeler, Robert (ed.) and Matthews, Alastair (Tr.), *German Invasion Plans for the British Isles, 1940 [Militärgeographische Angaben über England, 1940]* (Bodleian Library, 2007)

Williams, Penry, *Chetham's: Old and New in Harmony* (Manchester University Press, 1986)

Wright, Simon, *Memories of the Salford Blitz: Christmas 1940* (Neil Richardson, 1987)

Young, Richard Anthony, *The Flying Bomb* (Ian Allan, 1978)

VARIOUS DOCUMENTS

Manchester Council Emergency Committee Minutes 1939–44
(Greater Manchester Police Archives)

Manchester Emergency Committee's Log of Bombing Incidents
22–24 December 1940 (Greater Manchester Police Archives)

Salford Control Centre Air Raid Warning Messages (Salford Local
History Library)

Borough of Stretford Civil Defence Information 1941/1942
(Trafford Archives)

Report by Chief Fire Officer David Drummond to Manchester Fire Brigade
Sub Committee 16 January 1941 (GMFS Archives)

Metropolitan Vickers Committee of the Board Minute Book No. 6:
Aug 1940–Oct 1942 (Museum of Science and Industry)

Summarised Annual Reports by Trafford Park Estates Ltd 1939–40
(Collection Robert Nicholls)

Greater Manchester Fire Service Roll of Honour (GMFS Archives)

If the Invader Comes – What to Do and How to Do It (Ministry of Information)

*A Last Appeal to Reason by Adolf Hitler: Speech before the Reichstag,
19 July 1940* (Imperial War Museum Documents)

Kelly's Trade Directory 1940 (Manchester Local History Archives)

Victims of the V-1 Attack 24 December 1944, Abbey Hills Road, Oldham
(Oldham Local History Archives)

Bomb Damage in Stockport WWII (Stockport Reference Libraries)

Recommendations for Conditions in Air-Raid Shelters (HM Stationery
Office, September 1940)

Hansard 18 December 1940, 27 February 1941, 1 May 1941, 17 June 1941

The Lancet 14 December 1940: 'Shelter Deaths from Pulmonary Embolism'

Manchester Cathedral: A Short Tour – Official Cathedral Guide

MAPS

Luftwaffe reconnaissance map of Salford Docks and surrounding areas
August 1940 (Trafford Archives)

Record of location of aerial bombs on the City of Manchester
(Manchester Archives and Local Studies)

Salford bombing incidents 22–23 December 1940 (Salford Local
History Archives)

NEWSPAPERS

Manchester Evening News 1939–44
Manchester City News 1939–44
Manchester Guardian 1939–44, 1948
Spirit of Manchester: City News supplement 8 Feb 1941

Manchester Evening Chronicle 1939–44
Stretford and Urmston News 1940–41
The Stockport Advertiser 29 Dec 1944
Two Cities Go to War: MEN supplement 5 Sep 1989
The Oldham Evening Chronicle 20–21 Dec 1994, 3 Jan 1995
The Bury Times 31 Dec 2013

ORAL HISTORY RECORDINGS
Salford Life Times Oral History Collection
North West Sound Archive
Salford Quays Heritage

FILMS
Manchester Took It, Too (CWS 1941)
A City Speaks (Rotha Films 1946)
Both films are available to view at Archives Plus, Manchester Central Library

1940 Public Information Films may be viewed on the Internet:
    How You Can Deal with Incendiary Bombs
What to Do in an Air Raid, and *Your Home as an Air Raid Shelter*

WEBSITES
www.150.co-operative.coop *(search 'Blitz')*
www.wn.com/Manchester_blitz
www.salford.gov.uk *(LifeTimesLink)*
www.salfordwarmemorials.co.uk
www.traffordwardead.co.uk
www.aircrashsites.co.uk
www.mvbook.org.uk
www.levyboy.com
www.gracesguide.co.uk
www.hitlersukpictures.co.uk
www.telegraph.co.uk/history/world-war-two

INDEX OF PLACE AND STREET NAMES

Pubs and cinemas, and most factories, warehouses and shops, have been omitted from this Index. The reader should refer to the relevant street name, or the Appendices.

Page numbers in **bold** type refer to illustrations.

Key to districts and boroughs (if no district is given, the street or location is in the Manchester City Centre):

(An) =	Ancoats	(Lon) =	Longsight
(Ar) =	Ardwick	(Most) =	Moston
(AS) =	All Saints	(MP) =	Miles Platting
(Bes) =	Beswick	(MS) =	Moss Side
(Bla) =	Blackley	(NH) =	Newton Heath
(Bu) =	Borough of Bury	(Nor) =	Northenden
(Burn) =	Burnage	(Old) =	Borough of Oldham
(C-C-H) =	Chorlton-cum-Hardy	(OT) =	Old Trafford
(CheH) =	Cheetham Hill	(Pres) =	Prestwich
(Cla) =	Clayton	(Rus) =	Rusholme
(C-on-M) =	Chorlton on Medlock	(Sal) =	City of Salford
(Did) =	Didsbury	(Sto) =	Borough of Stockport
(Fal) =	Fallowfield	(Stra) =	Strangeways
(Gor) =	Gorton	(Stret) =	Stretford
(Har) =	Harpurhey	(TP) =	Trafford Park
(Hu) =	Hulme	(Tra) =	Borough of Trafford
(Hy) =	Hyde	(WhRa) =	Whalley Range
	(Borough of Tameside)	(Wi) =	Withington
(Lev) =	Levenshulme	(Wy) =	Wythenshawe